When
Jesus
Prayed

When Jesus Prayed

BRENDA POINSETT

BROADMAN PRESS
Nashville, Tennessee

4251-79
ISBN: 0-8054-5179-X

Dewey Decimal Classification: 232.9
Subject headings: JESUS CHRIST//PRAYER
Library of Congress Catalog Card Number: 80-67896
Printed in the United States of America

Acknowledgments

Without the help of three men, this book could not have been written. I'm indebted to B. H. Carroll, founding president of Southwestern Baptist Theological Seminary, William Barclay, author of the *Daily Study Bible,* and my husband, Bob Poinsett.

While researching my first book, *Prayerfully Yours,* I ran across two of Carroll's sermons on the prayers of Jesus. I knew then that I wanted to do an in-depth study of Jesus' prayers for my own enrichment and possibly for a book. When Broadman gave me the opportunity to write a book on Jesus' prayers, Carroll's sermons provided the basic framework for my research and the initial structure of the book.

When I write and when I teach Sunday School or Bible study groups, I'm always grateful to Barclay. His rich knowledge of the Greek and of the times in which Jesus lived are immensely helpful. Barclay makes the times and life of Jesus come so alive that I always feel closer to him after reading what Barclay has written.

But even with Carroll providing the structure and Barclay providing the background, the book still could not have been written without some practical assistance. My husband was my sounding board, my manuscript critic, and my breakfast cook (enabling me to write in the early-morning hours).

Carroll and Barclay have both gone to be with the Lord so, for the present, I cannot thank them; but I can thank my husband, and I do so by dedicating this book to him.

To
Bob Poinsett,
who might well be called Barnabas,
because he, too, is
"one who encourages"

Contents

We know not what we should pray
for as we ought . . . .
Lord, teach us to pray.
(Rom. 8:26; Luke 11:1)

1   Jesus' First Prayer

Did Jesus *need* to pray? The Bible tells us he prayed. This book is a study of his prayers. What we will receive from this study will depend on whether we believe Jesus needed to pray.

While many often give mental assent to the fact that Jesus was both God and man, most of them don't seem to believe it. They believe that the divine, so evident in his life, kept Jesus free and lifted him above the circumstances of life. He never knew how we really feel or what struggle is all about.

– With that kind of thinking, Jesus' prayers are sometimes interpreted as his baptism is. They are good examples for us to follow, but Jesus didn't really need them. If that is true, then the tears, the sweat, the agony, the withdrawal associated with Jesus' prayer life are only "props" for some very dramatic examples.

On the other hand, suppose Jesus needed to pray. Then the tears, the sweat, and the agony become real. The struggle becomes apparent. In recognizing this struggle and his need for prayer, we can identify with Jesus and find meaning for our own prayer life.

Examining Jesus' prayer life will not be easy. It's hard to examine anyone's prayer life because it is difficult to be certain about the thought processes of another person, even a contemporary, even a loved one. Entering the mind of someone who lived two thousand years ago and who was (and is) both God and man is even more difficult.

Our examination will be made easier when Jesus' actual prayers are stated. In some prayers we'll know exactly what he prayed for. At other times, the object of his prayer is not stated; it is inferred by the circumstances. Here our judgment will enter in. That is, we will determine the object of prayer by looking at what happened immediately following the prayer, by considering the events surrounding it, and by considering how we relate to the life of Jesus.

The first *recorded* prayer of Jesus' is an inferred prayer. It occurred at his baptism. John the Baptist had come out of the wilderness preaching repentance and forgiveness of sin (Luke 3:3). In recognition of their desire to repent and receive forgiveness of sin, many people were baptized by John. Although Jesus was without sin, he wanted to be baptized by John. As Jesus was being baptized, he prayed (Luke 3:21). For what was he praying?

Luke, who records this prayer, did not tell us what Jesus was praying for. Let us look at the evidence to see if we can determine the inferred object of prayer. Three things occurred after Jesus' prayer: (1) heaven was opened, (2) the Holy Spirit came down on Jesus in bodily form like a dove, and (3) a voice from heaven said, "Thou art my beloved Son; in thee I am well pleased" (Luke 3:22).

These three things are significant. The opening of heaven meant that God was about to reveal himself. The descent of the Holy Spirit in a bodily shape like a dove showed the coming of the Holy Spirit upon Jesus. The words spoken from heaven, composed of two texts from the Old Testament, directed Jesus' thoughts to the unusual combination of the messianic king and the Suffering Servant.

Jesus' baptism occurred at the beginning of his public ministry. While scholars speculate on reasons for Jesus' baptism, most agree that it marked the beginning of his earthly ministry. It is referred to by some as Jesus' "call" and by others as his "ordination." "The baptism of Jesus and the associated experience of the Spirit's descent constitutes his ordination for a ministry as Suffering Servant-Messiah. On his part, the baptism is his public commitment to God's will for his life."[1]

When we put the evidence together, we can make three conclusions about this prayer: (1) Jesus needed to hear from God; (2) he needed power; and (3) he needed to know where he was headed.

At some time in his youth, Jesus must have discovered his unique relationship to God. Surely he did not know it when he was a baby in the manger or as a small child, or he would have been a monstrosity. Luke said, "Jesus increased in wisdom" (2:52), and the writer of Hebrews said Jesus was perfected through his sufferings (5:8). A process was involved. Jesus had to come to know who he was and what he was to do.

Exactly when Jesus' consciousness of who he was began, we don't know. Maybe it began with the visit to the Temple when he was twelve (Luke 2:41-50). At his first Passover, on the brink of manhood, perhaps the realization began to dawn on him that he was not like other men.

By the time of the emergence of John the Baptist, Jesus was about thirty (Luke 3:23). Eighteen years had passed since the Temple visit. All through those years Jesus must have been thinking and realizing more and more his own uniqueness. While he worked as a carpenter, he must have known the day would come when he would say good-bye to his family and to Nazareth, his home, and go out into the world. He must have waited for some sign to tell him when to leave. When John the Baptist emerged and the people flocked to him, Jesus recognized the sign. It was time to commit himself.

"His baptism was probably the climax of a long period

of reflection, inner struggle, and deepening insight.''[2] In that sense, Jesus' baptism represented a turning point for him. One scholar even referred to it as a crisis. Either way, it was a significant moment in which Jesus needed God very much. By praying at his baptism, Jesus was seeking the Father. He needed him. Jesus knew that, above and beyond all human companionship, the deepest needs of his soul could only be known and met by God. Jesus might not have been asking for anything specific in this prayer, as much as he was asking for God himself. After periods of reflection, inner struggle, and deepening insight, Jesus might have felt as if his soul had been drained and had to be filled again with the strength of God.

Jesus needed God, and he needed God's power. Jesus knew that what was to follow could not be done in his own strength. He needed God's power in the form of the Holy Spirit to fulfill his destiny. B. H. Carroll wrote, "Feeling the magnitude of the work committed to him, as he was coming up out of the water, he prayed for the Holy Spirit, and the answer was instantly granted.''[3] The Holy Spirit came down upon Jesus in bodily form like a dove. Herbert Lockyer says Jesus could not have commenced his ministry without this prayer and the gift of the Holy Spirit.[4]

Why did Jesus need to ask for the Holy Spirit? Couldn't God have simply supplied the power since Jesus was going to do God's work? To answer that, we need to remember why we all need to ask. Our asking opens us to God, giving him the channels he needs to do, with us and through us, what he wants to do. It was not different for Jesus when he was on earth and limited by a human body. To suppose that his divineness freed him from operating under the limitations that we do is to undermine the truth of John 1:14: "And the Word [mind of God] was made flesh, and dwelt among us." Jesus was human. He was made like us; therefore, he needed to open his will to God just as any of us do in order to let God work through us.

Not only did Jesus need to know who he was and that he needed God and his power but he also needed to know if he were moving in the right direction. In answer to his prayer, God's voice came and acknowledged that Jesus was moving in the right direction. God mapped out Jesus' course by saying, "Thou art my beloved Son; in thee I am well pleased" (Luke 3:22). What God said is composed of two texts from the Old Testament which were very familiar to Jews and would, therefore, be familiar to Jesus.

"Thou art my Son" is from Psalm 2:7 and was always accepted as a description of the messianic king. "In whom my soul delights[I am well pleased]" is part of Isaiah 42:1. It is from a description of the servant of the Lord whose portrait culminates in the sufferings of Isaiah 53. To us those words are lovely but probably do not have much meaning. For Jesus, however, the words had meaning. Upon hearing them, he realized he was the Messiah, God's anointed King. He also realized that being the Messiah would involve not power and glory but suffering and a cross. William Barclay wrote, "The Cross did not come on Jesus unawares; from the first moment of realization He saw that Cross ahead. The baptism shows us Jesus asking for God's approval and receiving the destiny of the Cross."[5]

From the evidence surrounding Jesus' first recorded prayer, we can infer that Jesus needed God, he needed power, and he needed to know where he was going. Those inferences can remind us of some significant truths about prayer.

1. Prayer is more than asking for specific things. It is more than trying to use God as a source of favors and is more than emergency pleas. While asking for specific things is right, it shouldn't consume all of our praying. Prayer is also asking for someone.

There should come a time in every pray-er's life when prayer becomes, "More of you, God, more of you." Maybe this kind of prayer will come at a turning point, as it did in the life of Jesus. Maybe it will come at a time of crisis, at a time of loneliness, or at a time of recommitment. When the prayer comes is not as important as the fact that it does come when we seek God and not what God can give us.

2. Prayer is giving God the channel he needs to work through. It's opening our wills to him. Some Christians make the comment that if God wants them to have the Holy Spirit (or some other spiritual blessing), he will give it to them without their having to ask for it. But Jesus said, "How much more shall *your* heavenly Father give the Holy Spirit to them that ask him" (Luke 11:13). Jesus encouraged us to ask and to receive that our joy may be full (John 16:24). There are rich, spiritual blessings God wants to give us, but he can't until we open our wills to receive. Asking is the way we do that.

3. Prayer is a way of confirming God's direction in our lives. Many things help us determine God's will—the Bible, its stories of men and women and the guidelines it offers; mature Christians; the inward witness of the Holy Spirit; providential circumstances. Sometimes all of these intermingle in such a way that we "think" we know God's will. But, like Jesus, we need to take them to God, asking, "Am I right? Am I interpreting your will correctly?"

After praying, we wait then for the assurance to come, to be as indelibly printed on our hearts as the voice of God was on the ears of Jesus when he said, "Thou art my beloved Son; in thee I am well pleased."

We must understand though that while Jesus' destiny was confirmed for him with his baptism prayer, this occasion is not the last time we'll hear about it. A confirmation of direction for Jesus did not mean he would have no further struggle with God's will. Acceptance of the cross and more confirmation was needed. We'll see this as we look at the rest of Jesus' prayers. The destiny though will never change, and so all of his prayers will have to be seen in terms of God's will, namely the cross. When we examine Jesus' prayers in light of the cross, we're going to see struggle. Jesus was not immune from it, and we're going to see how very much he needed to pray.

Notes

1. *The Broadman Bible Commentary,* Vol. 9, Luke-John (Nashville, Tennessee: Broadman Press, 1970), p. 40.
2. Ibid.
3. B. H. Carroll, *Messages on Prayer,* J. W. Crowder, comp., J. B. Cranfill, ed. (Nashville, Tennessee: Broadman Press, 1942), p. 29.
4. Herbert Lockyear, *All the Prayers of the Bible* (Grand Rapids, Michigan: Zondervan Publishing House, 1959), p. 181.
5. William Barclay, *The Gospel of Luke,* Revised (Edinburgh, Scotland: The Saint Andrew Press, 1975), p. 33.

2　When Jesus Withdrew to Pray

Jesus needed to withdraw. That's the first apparent need we see in his prayer life. We do not have to look long at his life to see how much he needed time alone with the Father.

At the beginning of his ministry, Jesus spent a very busy sabbath in Capernaum. In the synagogue he amazed the people by casting out an unclean spirit (Mark 1:25). News about him and his ability spread quickly (Mark 1:28). Then Jesus healed Peter's mother-in-law (Mark 1:31), and that really did it! By sundown, people were bringing the sick and the demoniacs to Jesus for healing. The Bible says all the people of the town gathered in front of Peter and Andrew's house where Jesus was (Mark 1:33). Jesus read their hearts and sensed a crisis was developing.

Jesus knew the people were going to try to keep him from leaving. The multitude wanted to keep him in their place, concerned about their locality only. Jesus had to get alone to think and pray. After his long, exhausting day, Jesus left at daybreak and went to a solitary place to pray (Mark 1:35). Through prayer, Jesus came to understand clearly that he had to leave the miracle-seeking multitude and go to other places.

Soon Simon and those with him discovered that Jesus had disappeared. He had lingered long, and the multitudes were gathering again with their sick to be cured. They hunted him down and tried to keep him from leaving just as Jesus had sensed they would. "But he said to them, 'I must preach the Good News of the Kingdom of God in other towns also, because that is what God sent me to do' " (Luke 4:43, TEV).

Leaving Capernaum Jesus preached and healed in other cities of Galilee until the excitement again was irrepressible (Mark 1:40-45; Matt. 8:2-4; and Luke 5:12-16). It culminated with the cleansing of the leper whom Jesus commanded not to tell anyone, but who did anyway (Mark 1:45). This quite naturally attracted even greater crowds (Luke 5:15). How did Jesus handle this exploding popularity? Once again he withdrew to the wilderness and prayed (Luke 5:16).

When Jesus heard the news about the martyrdom of John the Baptist, he left the crowd and went by boat to a lonely place (Matt. 14:13). The news affected Jesus deeply. After all, through John's ministry Jesus had been baptized and had received direction for his own work in the world. Through his baptism, Jesus had learned that his ministry would involve conflict and danger. With John's death, Jesus probably realized the true implication of the path he had chosen. He knew that, like John, he would suffer and die for proclaiming the coming kingdom. Facing this realization called for solitude.

But Jesus would not remain alone for long. Galilee was a small, thickly populated country. It was difficult to get away from the crowds to be alone. It was quiet on the lake, and that is where Jesus went when he heard the news of John's death. But even then the crowd would not let him alone. They flocked around the shore on the other side of the lake, awaiting his arrival.

The waiting crowd, numbering over five thousand, lingered with Jesus as he healed their sick. Evening came, and they were hungry. Jesus miraculously provided food for them with five loaves and two fish. This miracle triggered a tremendous excitement among the people and the disciples. They wanted to take Jesus by force and make him a king (John 6:15). Jesus realized the crowd was getting to a point where it could not be controlled much longer. He dismissed the people and sent the disciples away. After he was alone, he went up into a mountain to pray (Mark 6:46).

In these four instances, we see that Jesus withdrew for several reasons. Jesus withdrew to escape the crowds and to deal with the pressures of popularity. He used his time alone to deal with shock and grief and to put things into their proper perspective. Jesus escaped to solitude and to refreshment with the Father.

Jesus did not take prayer lightly. For him, it was a necessity. Once he neglected the needy for a while in order to pray. The prayer on the mount of transfiguration is an example. When Jesus went up to the mountain to pray (Luke 9:28), most of the disciples remained behind. They continued to meet with and try to help the needy. Yet Jesus, Peter, James, and John avoided human need for a time when they went up into the mountain. When they came back down, the needy people were waiting for them.

Elton Trueblood says we need to remember that the quality of service depends primarily upon what we have to offer. We do not have enough to offer if we are always offering. "Christ left the needy people in order to engage in prayer, not because He did not care, but because He cared so much that He had to have times apart for conscious communion with the Father."[1]

Sometimes Jesus removed the disciples from the strain of human encounter. "There were so many people coming and going that Jesus and his disciples didn't even have time to eat. So he said to them, 'Let us go off by ourselves to some place where we will be alone and you can rest a while.' So they started out in a boat by themselves to a lonely place'' (Mark 6:31-32, TEV).

Busy people, especially those in the serving, healing, and teaching professions, need time alone. Continual giving drains us of our spiritual resources. These resources need to be replenished if we are to serve effectively.

Phillip Keller wrote *A Shepherd Looks at Psalm 23*. He believes that Christians who rise early each day to feed on God's Word and to pray are the ones most able to cope with life. It is in the quiet, early hours of the morning, he says, that Christians can imbibe the very life of Christ for the day.

Keller, being the shepherd, compares early morning Bible study and prayer to sheep rising just before dawn to start eating. In the early hours, the vegetation is drenched with dew—a clean, pure source of water. Sheep can keep fit on the amount of water taken in with their forage when they graze just before and after dawn. In fact, they can go for months without actually drinking, as long as they feed on the heavy dew each morning.

We Christians might not need so many group meetings to keep us going if more of us practiced withdrawal. We might not put so much pressure on our pastors to feed us if we were more adept at feeding ourselves. We will always need each other and our pastors, but we should never become dependent on either one or both to be the total source of our spiritual food. We need time apart to replenish our spiritual resources.

Bible study and prayer help us develop our personal relationships with God. When we become Christians, we begin our personal relationships with God. Unless we spend time with the Father and communication grows between us that relationship will stagnate. Stagnation occurs in a marriage if the partners refuse to talk to each other or are too busy for each other. In a friendship, the same thing can happen. Both parties must consciously work at the relationship. In the case of our relationship with God, we are always present to his mind. What we have to do is make God consciously present to ourselves. Withdrawal and prayer is the way to do this.

To make God consciously present to ourselves, we need to withdraw from other people and from the distractions of our work and responsibilities. We need time to talk to God and to listen to what he has to say. This is how the relationship develops. Being with God, talking to him, and listening as he responds is what withdrawal is all about. We may have to be just as deliberate about being apart with God as Jesus was. Withdrawal can serve as an impetus to keep us going.

An impetus is the force with which a moving body tends to maintain its velocity and overcome resistance. A Christian is surrounded by continual resistance in the form of spiritual warfare with the power of evil. Withdrawal can be our impetus to keep going and overcome the resistance. Some nights I go to bed weary from the struggle of living the Christian life, weary from bucking the continual resistance. The cares of this world hover around me like a thick cloud, and I think I can't make it through another day. But the next morning, I rise early and pray and feed on God's Word. God meets me in the experience, refreshing me. The cloud lifts, and strength comes to meet the day.

One person puts it this way, "At least periodically, it is necessary for me to withdraw from the routine of daily life, with its urgent demands on my attention. Obviously, such a withdrawal will have to be brief and temporary. Yet I will never come to pray in the fullest sense of that word unless I have opportunities to retire unto a place apart, undisturbed by the telephone, the social call, the television screen. It is not that these things do not have their proper place in life. But we shall be in a better position to see what that proper place is, by spending time away from them and alone with God."

The benefits of time alone with God cannot be stored up. We can't retreat for two weeks and expect that to last us for the year. The Hebrews in the desert had to gather their manna daily. We, too, must regularly withdraw to know the benefits of time with God.

While Jesus retreated for solitude and prayer when necessity demanded it, we should not conclude that those were the only times he prayed. Joachim Jeremias says the phrase "as his custom was" in Luke 4:16 may mean not only that he regularly attended the synagogue but also that he prayed regularly. In his early years, the silent years we call them, Jesus learned to pray and learned the Scriptures. Prayer and the Scriptures played a strong part in his ministry because he already knew their benefits.

If time alone with God is going to be meaningful for us, we need to make it habitual. Praying when we feel like praying or "when the Spirit moves us" is not the same thing. That kind of praying will never grow into the same kind of personal relationship that comes with appointed, set times to be with God. Spontaneous prayers do have a place in our life but they " . . . are richer and truer if they come out of a background of disciplined regularity. The best freedom is the freedom that emergest from a life of control."[2]

Rich prayers, true prayers, honest communion, and a close relationship with the Father were all part of Jesus' prayer life. They can be part of our prayers, too, once we see our need for time alone with God and make it a regular part of our lives.

Notes

1. Elton Trueblood, *The Lord's Prayers* (New York, Evanston and London: Harper and Row, 1965), p. 29.

2. Ibid., p. 28.

3   When Jesus Gave Thanks

Life is hard. At its best, life is still hard. To be involved in life is to be vulnerable to all the chances and changes that come with living. Jesus did not escape the harshness of life. He was made like us (Heb. 2:17); he was touched with the feeling of our infirmities (Heb. 4:15); he was tempted in all points as we are (Heb. 4:15); and he learned obedience through suffering (Heb. 5:8). What was Jesus' reaction? How did he respond to the realities of life?

Once a large group of men, five thousand in number, plus women and children gathered to be near him and to experience his healing power. The people stayed until it was time to eat. Jesus wanted to feed them. The disciples insisted they didn't have enough food to feed so many. " 'All we have here are five loaves and two fish,' they replied" (Matt. 14:17, TEV). Did Jesus change his desire in light of the limited resources? No, he organized the crowd, took the five loaves and two fish, looked up to heaven, and gave thanks. He then told the disciples to pass the food around. On another occasion (Matt. 15:32-39; Mark 8:1-10), Jesus did the same thing with seven loaves and a few small fish when four thousand men, plus women and children, needed food. The result? In both cases, there was more than enough food.

Jesus had to deal with all kinds of people. Naturally, he encountered those who made life difficult. Matthew 11

gives us a good example of the kind of perverse and cantankerous people Jesus had to sometimes put up with. He
mentioned those people who found fault with John the
Baptist. "This man is mad," they said. "He shouldn't cut
himself off from people and pleasure like he does." But
when Jesus came along, those same people said, "Jesus is
a socialite; he is the friend of outsiders no decent person
would have anything to do with."

Jesus mentioned the people living in the unbelieving
towns of Chorazin, Bethsaida, and Capernaum. He offered them the most precious thing in the world, and they
completely disregarded it. How did Jesus react to this kind
of treatment? He gave thanks: " 'Father, Lord of heaven
and earth! I thank you because you have shown to the
unlearned what you have hidden from the wise and
learned. Yes, Father, this was how you were pleased to
have it happen' " (Matt. 11:25-26, TEV).

This prayer was said on another occasion. The words
were then said with joy. "In that hour Jesus rejoiced in
spirit, and said, I thank thee" (Luke 10:21). What was
Jesus thrilled about? It must have had to do with what the
seventy had just learned. The seventy were followers of
Jesus whom he had sent out in twos to go ahead of him to
every town and place where he himself was about to go.
The seventy found, apparently to their surprise, that
people did listen and that healings actually occurred.
"Lord," they said, "even the demons obeyed us when we
gave them a command in your name!" (10:17). Jesus rejoiced with the seventy.

The most solemn prayer of thanksgiving was offered
when Jesus sat down with the twelve to keep the last
Passover meal. With profound emotion Jesus "took the
cup, and gave thanks" (Matt. 26:27). The fact that he was
instituting a way of remembrance for us doesn't take away
from the emotion it cost him at the time. We must remem-

ber that as Jesus gave thanks he was on his way to the cross, he was in the process of being betrayed, and he was about to be deserted by some of his closest friends.

The main point that emerges from these four references to Jesus' prayers of thanksgiving is that gratitude was an integral part of his prayer life, whether he was walking in the light or in the shadow. Thanksgiving leaped to his lips not just in life's shining hours. Indeed, it seems that praise poured forth from his heart especially in dark hours.

How can we get an attitude like Jesus'? How can we be thankful when walking in the light or in the shadow? How can we thankfully respond to the realities of life? Jesus' prayer life shows us how.

1. *Jesus related every experience to its ultimate source.* Jesus believed that everything that is, is because of God. Jesus made it a practice to relate every facet of creation to the Creator. This explains how he could see value and wonder in places, people, and events that others walked past in unawareness. One day in the midst of a crowd, some little children were clamoring to get closer to Jesus. In the judgment of the disciples, Jesus had more important people to see, so they shooed the children away. When Jesus saw what was happening, he said, "Suffer the little children to come unto me, and forbid them not" (Mark 10:14). Then Jesus placed his hands on them and prayed for them. It was his way of saying that these seemingly unimportant little ones did have value. Jesus took nothing for granted, nor regarded anything as worthless. Why? Because he saw all things in God; and, therefore, God in all things.

For us, it may take effort to relate every single experience with God. That's where the withdrawal, time apart, helps. Withdrawal is time spent in getting things in perspective. It is spending time taking stock of one's situation. We do not see "things" to be thankful for unless we develop a sensitivity (sometimes called a sense of wonder) about life. It's not that God did not originally give us a sense of wonder. We possessed it as children, but somewhere on the way to adulthood, we lost it. Maybe it's the process of trying "to make it" or "just keeping our heads above water" that makes us grow cynical and lose our sense of wonder. To avoid this, we need to regularly take time to put life in its proper perspective.

2. *Jesus trusted in God's ways.* Jesus not only possessed a sense of reality but he also believed in the nearness and the sufficiency of God. Nothing, he felt, was too wonderful to happen in the same world as God. Events which seem to us to be no great affairs were important to him. As we judge the mission of the seventy, it was at most and best only a tiny dent in the mass of evil in the world. Jesus, however, met the seventy with a cry of triumph. "I saw Satan fall like lightning from heaven" (Luke 10:18, TEV), he declared.

Often in a person's prayers his truest thoughts about himself and about God come to the surface. For this reason, says one scholar, the thanksgiving of Jesus recorded in Matthew 11:25-26 is one of the most precious pieces of spiritual autobiography to be found. It shows that the main characteristic of Jesus' life was obedience to his Father's will. "A wonderful self-effacement and self-surrender underlies the words *for so it seemed good in thy sight.* They bear eloquent testimony to the truth that *whatever* the Father's gracious will might be, it was accepted without question by His Son, even if humanly speaking acceptance might involve him in much disappointment and distress."[1]

3. *Jesus trusted in God's nature.* Before saying the word of power at the grave of Lazarus, Jesus lifted up his eyes to heaven and said, "Father, I thank thee that thou hast heard me. And I knew that thou hearest me always" (John

11:41-42). Clearly, Jesus had already prayed for Lazarus to be raised from the dead. In this prayer at the grave, in front of the gathered crowd and *before the actual evidence of the resurrection*, Jesus thanked God. After the prayer, he commanded Lazarus to come forth. Jesus was acting in accordance with God's nature. Jesus knew that God is true to his nature; it is God's nature to answer prayer, and Jesus acted accordingly. Lazarus came forth.

On the occasions of the feeding of the five thousand and the feeding of the four thousand, we see Jesus acting in accord with the providential side of God's nature. Some writers, in commenting on the miraculous feedings, say that Jesus' prayers of thanks had nothing to do with the miracles. While the words of thanks might not have directly produced the miracles, the acts of thanksgiving did play a part. Jesus' resources were limited, but he knew God's providential nature. Jesus' act of thanksgiving and his use of what resources he had in hand show a remarkable confidence in God's ability to provide.

For most of us, having confidence in God's nature is a goal to work toward. We seem to spend the better part of our Christian life trying to convince ourselves that God is trustworthy. Immersing ourselves in the Bible where we can discover his nature for ourselves helps. We should fill our minds with what God is like until his nature is fixed on our minds. We need to trust God to the extent that we can say, "I thank thee, Lord, that thou hast already heard me." When we trust God like that, we can thank God even when we can't see that our prayers have been answered.

4. *Thanksgiving played a major role in the prayer life of Jesus.* When the two discouraged disciples met Jesus on the road leading to Emmaus, they did not know him. After chatting with him for a while, they invited Jesus to share a meal with them (Luke 24:30-31). During the blessing and as the food was passed around the table, the eyes

of the two disciples were opened, and they recognized him.

What was it that triggered the opening of their eyes? Interestingly enough, they recognized Jesus when he sat down to eat with them. He picked up a simple loaf of bread, blessed it, and broke it. They remembered other times of thanksgiving—the breaking of five small loaves, the handling of small children, the passing of a cup of wine—and recognized the stranger in their midst.

The disciples had never known anyone else to take something as commonplace as a piece of bread and treat it with such wonder and gratitude. They had never seen anybody make thanksgiving such a prominent part of prayer, as Jesus did. Therefore, it is not surprising that this act of giving thanks triggered their recognition of Jesus. They realized Jesus was alive and still giving thanks for the simple things of life.

Most of us don't ask, Is thanksgiving a dominant part of my prayer life? Rather, our question is, How can I make thanksgiving a dominant part of my prayer life? Unless we already possess a sense of wonder or unless thanksgiving comes naturally for us, it will take some effort.

Some pray-ers make it a practice to begin all their prayers with thanksgiving. This increases the role of thanksgiving. Even if these people do not enter their prayer time with a "thanks" already on their minds, they do not make one request until some thanks has been uttered. That amounts to "taking stock" of things to be thankful for. One pray-er who tried this for the first time found a change within herself in a period of one week. She said, "After a few days of praying this way, I saw how selfish I had been in my praying. For years, I had been caught up with my requests and what I needed and failed to give God credit for what he was doing in my life."

While this step of beginning all prayers with thanks-

giving sounds simple, it is not always easy for pray-ers to
put it into practice. A lot of times when working with
small groups, we pray together conversationally. I ask the
participants not to make any requests until I indicate the
appropriate time. I say, "For the first few minutes, let's
just give thanks and praises." There are always those participants who can't do it, who cannot pray without asking.
Now, prayer *is* for asking; it is right to ask, but prayer is
also for thanksgiving. We need to practice giving God the
recognition he so rightly deserves.

One way to make the effort is to begin our prayers with
thanksgiving. Other Christians, a little farther along in
their pilgrimages, thank God for his answers before they
come. They've caught the spirit of Jesus thanking God for
always hearing, as he did at the tomb of Lazarus.

Other pray-ers give God thanks in every situation (1
Thess. 5:18). They are consistent in doing this, no matter
what comes their way and no matter how they feel. They
base their thanks on God's nature and not on whether they
feel grateful.

At first glance, putting such effort into our thanksgiving seems to be in direct contrast with Jesus' thanksgiving. His was so natural. He could pray in the middle of
a crowd or alone. There was no pious wind-up—no let-us-
pray preliminary. He simply said, "I thank thee, Father."
Jesus just seemed to burst forth in thanks. For example,
so real and simple is the conversation between Jesus and
the Father that one hardly knows where the prayer ends
and conversation with the seventy begins. (Compare different translations of Luke 10:21-22 and note where the
quotation marks are placed.)

We must remember, however, that Jesus related everything to God. He trusted God's ways. He trusted in God's
nature. We're not always at that point when we pray. But
if we want thanksgiving to be a major part of our prayer

lives, we can *act* upon those truths. We can make ourselves give thanks regardless of how we feel or how difficult saying thanks might be for us. We can verbally relate everything to God and show by our prayers that his ways and nature can be trusted. When we make ourselves give thanks, we are acting on the truth of what Jesus naturally accepted.

Will it do any good to go ahead and make ourselves give thanks even when we don't feel like it? Giving thanks won't alter our circumstances, will it?

Sometimes it will. One woman began giving thanks for her cantankerous husband. She praised God for her husband, for his ability to provide, and for his faithfulness. Without her saying anything to her husband, his personality mellowed in response to her changed attitude. Saying thanks changed her attitude, and her changed attitude changed her husband.

But truthfully, sometimes the circumstances do not change—at least not right away. Circumstances may not be altered by our thanksgiving, but our attitudes will be. That can make all the difference in the way we live with the circumstances. Jesus could have said, "Well, let people be people. If they choose to ignore me, that's their problem." But he didn't. He responded with thanksgiving and consequently was able to see God in his circumstances. "For so it seemed good in thy sight" was his conclusion.

Once we begin to practice thanksgiving in the face of the realities of life, we can begin to see God's hand in life. We begin to see the possibility of purpose behind the circumstances and the possibility of good coming out of what we are enduring. The facts may still be the same, but we won't be the same. That will make all the difference in our ability to cope.

Sometimes, Christians who practice giving thanks in

every situation almost appear to other Christians and especially to the world as naive. They appear to be Pollyannas, blindly optimistic and unscathed by the realities of life. In actuality, this isn't true. Often underneath, in their past, they have handled some severe blows. But they determinedly give thanks and maintain their sense of wonder. In return, God blesses them and gives them his peace to stand guard over their hearts.

Paul told us about this peace. When he asked the Philippians to make all of their prayers and supplications with thanksgiving, he said the result will be that the peace of God would "keep" their hearts and minds (4:6-7). The Greek word that Paul used, which the King James Version translates "keep," is *phrourein,* a military word for *standing on guard.* Paul described this peace as surpassing all human thought.

William Barclay says this means that the peace of God is so precious that man's mind, with all its skill and all its knowledge and all its understanding, can never contrive it, find it, or produce it. This peace is utterly beyond man's ability to obtain by himself. It can never be of man's contriving; it is only of God's giving. The way to this kind of peace is to take ourselves and all of life, including its harsh realities, and place them trustingly and thankfully in the hands of God. So what may be interpreted as naiveté on the part of some is really the peace of God standing guard.

To be sure, thanksgiving never took away the cross from Jesus. Thanksgiving is not a method to be used in an attempt to manipulate God into giving us what we want. Thanksgiving is an attitude to be developed to give us the insight and peace necessary to handle the realities of life.

Notes

1. Leon Morris, *The Gospel According to St. Luke,* Vol. III, *Tyndale New Testament Commentaries* (Grand Rapids, Michigan: William B. Eerdmans Publishing Company, 1974), p. 121.

4   When Jesus Had to Choose

Choices aren't always easy to make, even for Christians. Turning points come to all of us when we must decide, Which way now? or, What do I do? or, How do I handle this? Jesus, too, faced turning points—decisions upon which the continuation of his ministry and message depended. Let's see what Jesus did when he had to choose.

A crisis occurred for Jesus when the Pharisees began to plot against him. The Pharisees had accused Jesus' disciples of breaking scribal rules by plucking wheat on the sabbath. Furthermore, they were "filled with madness" because Jesus had healed a man on the sabbath (Luke 6:11). Filled with rage, they began to discuss among themselves what they would do to Jesus. They entered into what was for them an "unholy alliance" with the Herodians, and together they plotted to kill Jesus.

The opposition reminded Jesus that death lay ahead. The lines of battle had been drawn; the dangers for Jesus were increasing daily. In Nazareth an attempt had been made on his life. There he had been hustled to the hilltop in order to be hurled down, but had escaped (Luke 4:29). This new desire to see him killed reminded Jesus that his time for accomplishing his mission of earth was limited. Jesus came to the grim realization that if he continued his work he risked a fate similar to John the Baptist's.

Not only was Jesus limited by time but also he was lim-

ited by space. He could only be in one place at a time. His
voice could reach only a limited number of people. In that
day there were no means of mass communication. If any
message was presented to people, it was presented personally. If his work was to go on, Jesus needed help. He
needed men to go where he could not go and to speak
where he could not speak.

Who would these men be? Jesus had followers but what
he needed were men who would commit themselves to
him. He needed men who would love him, who would try
to understand his purpose and task, and who would be
willing to help him carry it out. Out of his followers, he
had to choose men on whose hearts and lives he could
write his message and who would go out from his presence
to carry that message abroad.

It was not an easy choice to make. Because Jesus was
making the choice and because we know the outcome of
the choice, we tend to underestimate the difficulty of the
choice for Jesus. There is every reason to believe that
Jesus took this task seriously. Elton Trueblood calls this
decision to select the apostles one of the crucial decisions
of the world. "There is no reason to suppose that we
should ever have heard of the gospel apart from this carefully conceived step. Without this step the teaching of
Christ might easily have been . . . ''[1] a bubble which
eventually burst. Gamaliel, a respected Pharisee, told
about two bubbles which did eventually burst. He told of
two, would-be messiahs who were killed and whose work
did not continue on (Acts 5:36-37). If this were not to happen to the work of Jesus, then he needed men to carry on
his teachings. So, his choice of who those men would be
was, indeed, a crucial one.

The crowd might be there one day and gone the next.
Followers might come and go. They might fluctuate and
be spasmodic in their attachment to Jesus, but Jesus

needed some men who were willing to identify their lives with his. How did Jesus go about choosing such men?

In light of the crucial nature of the decision, it is not surprising that Jesus faced this particular choice with prayer. "At that time Jesus went up a hill to pray and spent the whole night there praying to God. When day came, he called his disciples to him and chose twelve of them, whom he named apostles" (Luke 6:12-13, TEV).

Curtis Mitchell says the language in the original text clearly indicates that the only reason Jesus took the trouble to climb that mountain was to pray. He did not go out for a hike up the mountain and then decide it would be nice to pray. Alone and apart from the distractions of the world, Jesus let his mind and soul commune with God. He sought guidance and illumination about the momentous decision he had to make.

The Bible says Jesus prayed "all night" about this decision (Luke 6:12). The word translated "all night" is a medical term. It was used in the Greek to describe the all-night vigil of a doctor as he waited at the bedside of a patient. The original word gives a picture of urgency, earnestness, and intensity.

We are not saying that Jesus was petitioning God with words all night long. As one writer said, "He was revealing what prayer at its most intense can be: an undistracted listening to God." The decision was crucial. Long hours of prayer were required in order to know the Father's will in the matter of choosing apostles.

What kind of answer did Jesus receive after his long hours of prayer? What kind of men did God direct him to choose? Jesus chose twelve apostles from the disciples who had been with him the longest. He chose twelve ordinary men. They were not wealthy, famous, or influential. They had no special education. They were not trained theologians; they were not high-ranking churchmen. They belonged to the simple, unlearned class of people whose minds were relatively unhindered by the traditions of the rabbis. In the choice, there was no regard for social position, political party, or religious sect.

The twelve apostles were also a strange mixture. Some of them were fishermen by trade. One was a tax collector, an outcast who was looked upon as a traitor by his fellow Jews. Another was a Zealot. The Zealots were fanatical nationalists, men who were sworn to kill every traitor and every Roman they could lay their hands on.

Judging them by worldly standards, the men Jesus chose had no special qualifications, yet Jesus saw in these men the ones who would be willing to accept him as their master. He saw them as courageous men. Jesus was branded a sinner and a heretic; the opposition was determined to get him. They would have to be courageous just to travel with him.

These twelve men had all kinds of faults; but because they were courageous and willing to follow, Jesus would be able to use them. God's answer to Jesus' prayer seems surprising to us. Certainly, these were not the kind of men we would look for to fill important positions. It was a surprising answer; but because it was God's answer, Jesus was assured that these twelve ordinary men would be able to change the world.

Hard decisions are agonizing to thoughtful, conscientious Christians who want to do the right thing. Studying how Jesus faced his crisis that demanded a choice can help us in making our choices.

This crisis in Jesus' life reminded him that he was limited by time and space. Because of those limitations he needed men to help him if his mission and message were to survive. But who would those men be? The nature of Jesus' choice was selecting the appropriate men for the job. The crisis helped him recognize the need for a decision.

Every decision has its alternatives, and all those alternatives need to be considered before a sound decision can be made. What if Jesus had not decided on a small group of twelve men? What if he had chosen others than those he did? Elton Trueblood says, "Christ could have avoided the choosing of the Twelve; He could have chosen others than the ones whose names we know. How different the world might be in consequence!"[2]

For every road taken, there is "the road not taken." The choices and their consequences need to be carefully considered before a decision is made. Each alternative should be followed to its logical end, considering all the possibilities. If we choose without exploring all the possibilities, we might end up angry with God. "You led me to do this; now look what a mess I am in!" No decision is foolproof in the sense that success and perfection are guaranteed. Jesus' choice included the apostle that would later betray him.

Once we know the nature of our decision and have followed its alternatives through to their logical ends, we need to do the same thing Jesus did. We need to maintain a vigil of prayer. Maintaining a vigil of prayer doesn't necessarily mean spending one night in prayer. Decisions that are crucial, involving far-reaching consequences, need to be faced in long hours of effort in order to know what God's will is. This may take days or even weeks. When the choice is between good and evil, God's voice seems to be loud and clear. But when it comes to choosing between "good" alternatives, his voice does not seem to have the same volume. In order to hear God's voice directing us, we need to withdraw to a place alone and eliminate all distractions.

One word of warning is needed here. God's answer to our prayers may be surprising. While the promise that God will answer is a surety, *how* he will answer is unpredictable.

While I was in seminary, a prominent pastor told of his burden to reach the young people of his community. He thought recreation was the way to reach them, so he gathered some plans for a recreation building which included a skating rink, bowling alley, and the like. He knew he would have no problem getting his congregation to back the plan and pay for the building. But, almost as an afterthought, he decided to put away the plans for awhile and pray for God's direction on how to reach the young people. God's answer was a surprise. He led the pastor to establish Bible study-fellowship groups throughout the community to reach the young people. The idea worked, and the idea of the recreation building was permanently tabled.

God's ways are not our ways (Isa. 55:8); he may have a different way of doing things than we do. This is not to say that we always plan contrary to God's will. The pastor could have received a green light from God about the building. Either way he could have carried on with assurance, knowing he was doing it God's way. He had prayed and listened for God's direction just as Jesus did when he had to choose his apostles.

Notes

1. Elton Trueblood, *The Lord's Prayers,* p. 36.
2. Ibid., p. 38.

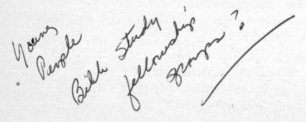

5   When Jesus Prayed for Recognition

"And it came to pass, as he was alone praying, his disciples were with him: and he asked them, saying, Whom say the people that I am?" (Luke 9:18). We are not told what Jesus was praying for on this occasion, but we can infer the object of prayer from the circumstances.

Jesus was well into the last year of his ministry. The great Galilean ministry had ended. Jesus never again taught the people around the Sea of Galilee. Later he passed through Galilee on his way to Jerusalem, but his ministry there was over.

The opposition of the Jewish leaders had greatly increased in intensity, and Jesus was well aware of it. He saw, too, that he was surrounded by an atmosphere of hatred. He knew that in the end his enemies would take his life. The certainty of the cross lay ahead.

This was also a time of discouragement for Jesus. Matthew describes the dullness of the disciples after nearly three years under Jesus' teaching (16:5-12). It was a time of doubt on the part of his followers. Many who had followed Jesus now left him. His popularity among the ordinary people was still quite strong; though it, too, was beginning to decline.

The danger he was in and the discouragement he experienced with his followers confronted Jesus with a question which demanded an answer, Did anyone recognize him?

Had anyone really discovered who he was? "His Kingdom was a kingdom within the hearts of men, and, if there was no one who had enthroned him within his heart, then his Kingdom would have ended before it ever began. But if there was some one who had recognized him and who understood him, even if as yet inadequately, then his work was safe."[1]

Jesus had to find an answer to the question, "Does anyone recognize me?" "The answer would make all the difference. If there was no answer, but dull incomprehension, it meant that all his work had gone for nothing. If there was an answer of realization, however incomplete, it meant that he had lit such a torch in the hearts of men as time would never put out."[2]

To find the answer, Jesus had to take his disciples away for a brief time from the tensions and threats which surrounded them. Jesus needed to be alone with them and led them to Caesarea Philippi.

Legend had it that all the gods gathered at Caesarea Philippi. Scattered around the area were the temples of Baal worship; fourteen were in the immediate vicinity. Nearby was the hill and cave said to be the birthplace of the great god Pan. The great temple of white marble built to the godhead of Caesar was also located there. As Jesus and his disciples met in the shadow of the ancient gods, they were within sight of where Israel had worshiped the golden calf. Against this background, Jesus prayed. He prayed that his disciples would be able to discern what was true. He prayed that they would be able to recognize him.

After praying, Jesus began to question his disciples. First, he asked, "Who do the crowds say I am?"

Several answers were given as the disciples began to quote what others were saying about Jesus. "Some say John the Baptist." Here they were probably quoting Herod's terrified opinion. Herod was scared that Jesus was a ghost sent to haunt him for murdering John the Baptist.

"Others say Elijah." Elijah had been taken up without dying, and Malachi said Elijah would return again. Perhaps Jesus was Elijah.

"Others say Jeremiah." Some thought according to 2 Maccabees 2, Jeremiah would return and reveal the place of the tabernacle, ark, and altar of incense.

"One of the prophets" was another answer. This wasn't a haphazard guess, but a compliment. For, if the people regarded Jesus as a prophet, they regarded him as a man within the confidence of God (Amos 3:7).

Actually, all of these answers were intended to be compliments, but that was not what Jesus wanted. Jesus did not accept the verdicts of the crowd, and he pressed for a deeper answer. "What about you?" he asked them. "Who do you say I am?"

Peter, answering for himself and the others, cried out, "Thou art the Christ, the Son of the living God" (Matt. 16:16). The heart of Jesus must have glowed with happiness. By Peter's answer, Jesus knew he had not failed. His prayer was answered, and in his exultation, he said, "Blessed art thou, Simon Barjona: for flesh and blood hath not revealed *it* unto thee, but my Father which is in heaven" (Matt. 16:17). Jesus acknowledged that the confession had been supernaturally given. He acknowledged God's gracious answer to his need for recognition as he had expressed it in prayer to the Father.

Jesus could have just told the disciples who he was. He could have preached it to them. He could have repeated it and repeated it until they could spit out the right answer for him. But their discovery was an answer to his prayer. Thus the moment was more meaningful than if Jesus had just told them who he was. The confession was for Jesus a confirmation that God was still at work in his life. Jesus needed that confirmation very much at this point in his life.

By discovery, through the process of asking and answering, the confession was also more meaningful for the disciples. The lessons that stay with us the longest are those we discover. Truth has a double impact when it is a personal discovery. So a good teacher will provide the atmosphere and the stimulation needed to enable his students to make discoveries of their own. Sets of facts can be memorized; tests can be crammed for; but those things which stay with us and produce change in our lives are those things we personally discover.

Jesus' prayer for recognition departs from what we have studied so far about his prayer life. For one thing, the Bible says, "as he was alone praying, his disciples were with him" (Luke 9:18). This withdrawal was different because he was not completely alone. This could mean that he was in a solitary spot apart from the disciples but could see them. Perhaps his praying in their presence led them to believe that his praying was intended to have an effect on them. They were, therefore, prepared for the questions which followed.

On the other hand, prayer seminar leader Don Miller looks upon the disciples' presence while Jesus was praying as insulation. Perhaps they were protecting Jesus from those forces which were against him or from the constant demands made upon him, thus enabling him to pray.

Either way, Jesus' praying in the presence of others shows us that we do not always have to be alone to pray effectively. While solitude will often be preferable for prayer, God can and will answer prayers said under less than ideal situations. We can be alone with God and be with people at the same time. We can close our minds to distractions around us without having to close our eyes in prayer. Waiting for a perfect time and place is never a good reason for putting off praying.

A second thing that is unusual about this prayer for recognition is the answer. The answer from the disciples was not perfect, but it was sufficient.

Jesus was joyful that Peter recognized him as the Christ, the Messiah. Peter and the other disciples did not fully comprehend what it meant for Jesus to be the Messiah. When Jesus tried to explain what it meant for him to be the Messiah, Peter began to rebuke him (Matt. 16:22). Jesus connected being the Messiah with suffering and death. To the disciples his statements were both incredible and incomprehensible. All their lives they had thought of the Messiah in terms of irresistible conquest, and now Jesus presented ideas which staggered them. Advanced as Peter's insight was, he immediately rejected the idea of a suffering Messiah (Matt. 16:22-23).

At Caesarea Philippi, Jesus had the joy of knowing that his work was safe because at least one person understood. But at Caesarea Philippi, Jesus knew that he still had the problem of making those who loved him fully understand. He had to teach the disciples that he was to be a suffering Messiah. He had to show them plainly that he had to go to Jerusalem, be rejected, suffer, and die for his people. In the sense that Jesus still had more work to do with regard to recognition, the answer to his prayer was not as yet completed.

The answer, though, was sufficient. It gave Jesus the reassurance he needed: his close followers were beginning to perceive who he really was; he had indeed ignited a torch in their hearts which would never go out. While the flame might have been very small at this time, it was strong enough to serve as a springboard for Jesus to teach his disciples the truth about the future.

We can learn some helpful things from Jesus' prayer for recognition and the answer he received. If we take them to heart, they can eliminate a lot of frustration from our praying and from the answers we receive.

1. God's answer will be sufficient. That's a great consolation. The answer may not be specifically what we have asked for, but it will be sufficient to meet our needs. Harry Emerson Fosdick says God will either change the circumstances in response to our prayer or he will supply sufficient power to overcome them. God answers either the petition or the man.

This truth explains such amazing statements as Adoniram Judson, for example, made at the close of his life: "I never prayed sincerely and earnestly for anything, but it came; at some time—no matter at how distant a day— somehow, in some shape—probably the last I should have devised—it came." But Judson had prayed for entrance into India and had been compelled to go to Burma; he had prayed for his wife's life, and had buried both her and his two children; he had prayed for release from the King of Ava's prison and had lain there months, chained and miserable. Scores of Judson's petitions had gone without an affirmative answer. But *Judson* always had been answered. He had been upheld, guided, reenforced; unforeseen doors had opened through the very trials he sought to avoid; and the deep desires of his life were being accomplished not in his way but beyond his way.[3]

2. God's answer may not be complete in the sense that there will no longer be any struggle to what we were praying about. Too many of us want answers to prayers that will mean the end of our struggles, but struggle is a part of life. It is unrealistic to expect most of our problems to be eliminated by one swooping answer to prayer. God will answer and answer sufficiently, but that answer doesn't necessarily mean the end of the struggle. It wasn't until the resurrection that the disciples finally recognized Jesus as who he really was and what being the Messiah really meant.

3. God's answer is not to be viewed as an isolated incident but as part of an ongoing process. Jesus was on his way to the cross. His destiny was to be the suffering Messiah. No amount of praying would change that. His dying on the cross was a voluntary act; but, in another sense, it wasn't. If he wanted to be the obedient Son, there was only one way before him. His destiny was an unchangeable certainty.

Some of us face unchangeable certainties—things we must live with that all of the praying in the world will not remove. While we are able to control many things in this world by our actions, prayers, attitudes, and so forth, some things which happen to us are beyond our control. A flash flood comes without warning in the middle of the night; in what seems like minutes, the possessions of many families are washed away. A deranged killer walks into a Sunday morning church service and fires random shots into the audience, killing five church members. A car driven by a drunken driver crosses the median and hits a car carrying a Christian family on their way to church— the father and youngest child are killed instantly. After the fact, these events cannot be changed. They are fixed and we have to pick up the fragments of life and go on.

The flood and the deaths are unchangeable certainties in the past. Jesus' future was an unchangeable certainty. Some of us face that kind of certainty, too, not that a cross is waiting before us—but a destiny is. God may be calling us to a particular task or vocation that, at first, our nature wants to avoid; but if we want to be obedient children, then we don't really have a choice.

However, we do have prayer. It may not remove the unchangeable certainty from our life, but it will help us live with it. Jesus continually brought his needs with regard to his destiny to God through prayer. His need was for recognition. God granted him the recognition he needed. God's answer did not mean the end of struggle, but it was sufficient for the moment.

Notes

1. William Barclay, *The Mind of Jesus* (New York: Harper and Row, 1960, 1961), p. 167.

2. William Barclay, *The Gospel of Luke,* p. 120.

3. Harry Emerson Fosdick, *The Meaning of Prayer* (New York: Association Press, 1915), pp. 130-131.

6 When Jesus Prayed for Confirmation

After Peter's confession, it was time for Jesus to tell the disciples of his impending death, which was just a little over six months away. "From that time forth," the Bible says, Jesus began revealing in plain, matter-of-fact statements what lay ahead. First, he told them he had to go to Jerusalem (Matt. 16:21). Second, he had to suffer many things at the hands of the elders, chief priests, and scribes (Matt. 16:21; Mark 8:31; and Luke 9:22). The third thing he told them was the plain, rude, shocking fact of his death. He had to be killed. (Jesus still hadn't mentioned the cross. The fact of his death had to be revealed first.) Finally, Jesus attempted to relieve the dark message of death by the bright hope of the resurrection. He would be raised up on the third day, but the disciples did not catch that hope. "These four things Jesus had to go over and over again with the disciples, to try to get them to understand. Even then they but poorly comprehended."[1]

All through Jesus' ministry there had been half-veiled intimations about the necessity of his dying. None of these symbolic references had been fully understood by the disciples who were filled with the current Jewish conceptions about the Messiah. That their Messiah would suffer was entirely foreign to the Jews' way of thinking. He was to be a conqueror.

If you have ever tried to change someone's mind about

set concepts, particularly in the religious realm, you know what a difficult task lay before Jesus. Sometimes the trying can discourage us so much that we begin to wonder if we are right. Is what I am proposing really the truth? Trying to teach the disciples what the true Messiah was like must have been an unsettling experience for Jesus, for about a week after he began his hard, clear teaching, he departed for prayer (Luke 9:28).

Luke is the only Gospel writer to tell us the subject of Jesus' praying: he was praying about "his decease which he should accomplish at Jerusalem" (Luke 9:31). Jesus needed the confirmation that he was, indeed, right about God's will for his life—that he was to go to Jerusalem. How did he go about seeking this confirmation? He went up the mountain to pray.

While Jesus was praying, his face changed apearance, and his clothes became dazzling white (Luke 9:29). God confirmed his will for Jesus through Elijah and Moses, through the cloud, and through his own voice.

Moses and Elijah appeared to Jesus and talked with him about the way in which he would fulfill God's purpose by dying in Jerusalem (Luke 9:31). Moses and Elijah were the two supreme figures of Jewish religion. Moses was the supreme lawgiver, and Elijah was the supreme prophet. Jesus was very aware that his concept of Messiah was completely different from the popular conception, but here Moses and Elijah encouraged him to go on. "It is as if they said to him: 'It is you who are right, and it is the popular teachers who are wrong; it is you in whom there is the fulfilment of all that the law says and all that the prophets foretold. The real fulfilment of the past is not in the popular idea of might and power, but in your way of sacrificial love.' "[2]

The appearance of Elijah and Moses woke Peter, John, and James who had accompanied Jesus to the mountain to pray and sparked a conversation between Peter and Jesus. While they were talking, a cloud appeared and covered them with its shadow. All through the history of Israel there is the idea of the *shechinah*. The *shechinah* is the glory of God. Again and again this glory appeared to the people in the form of a cloud. And, now the glory of God was upon Jesus, assuring him and showing the disciples God's approval on what he was doing.

Out of the cloud came the voice of God. "This is my beloved Son: hear him" (Mark 9:7). Those words remind us of the words God spoke to Jesus at his baptism, another time in which he needed the Father's direction. In the Greek, those words go something like this: "This is my Son, the dearly-beloved one; be constantly hearing him." God was confirming the rightness of Jesus' interpretation of himself and of what it means to follow him. With the appearance of Moses and Elijah, with the *shechinah* glory, and most of all, with the voice of God himself, Jesus knew he could and would go on to do what must be done.

Instead of seeing this prayer as Jesus' seeking God's confirmation, B. H. Carroll sees it as Jesus praying that his followers see a glimpse of his glory, lest they should be depressed by views of his humiliation. Carroll says Jesus' followers were depressed by all the humiliation Jesus would suffer. The transfiguration of Jesus would go far toward reconciling their minds to what before had been so abhorrent.

The transfiguration was a help to the disciples. The minds of Peter, James, and John were bewildered by the insistence of Jesus that he must go to Jerusalem to suffer and to die. It must have looked to them as if there were nothing but shame ahead. But the whole atmosphere of the transfiguration is glory. Jesus' face shone like the sun. His garments glistened and gleamed like the light. No Jew would have seen that luminous cloud without thinking of the glory of God resting upon his people. Surely here was something which would lift up the hearts of the disciples. Here was something that would enable them to see the glory through the shame and humiliation. Even though they did not fully understand, it must have given them hope to know that not all would be humiliation; there would be glory as well.

There isn't any reason why we can't accept both explanations for this prayer. After all, Jesus did spend the night in prayer—long enough to cover more than one matter of concern. And he did take Peter, James, and John with him. He surely wanted them there for a reason.

How can this prayer, which helped Jesus and helped the disciples, help us? It can help us in two ways: (1) by encouraging us to pray for confirmation of God's will, and (2) by encouraging us to ask for a glimpse of glory when the going gets rough.

At times a little of Gideon comes out in all of us; we need the confirmation that what we are doing is God's will. This is especially true when all the circumstances around us seem to be pointing contrary to God's will. That's when we need to pray, "Father, have I interpreted your will correctly?"

For a long time, I felt God had called me to be a writer. But the many rejection slips I received certainly seemed to indicate otherwise. I remember one project in particular. I had worked with great intensity at what I had felt was God's initiative and direction. When the project was rejected, I was baffled as to what this meant concerning God's leadership. "God," I prayed, "if you want me to continue to write, I pray that at least one of the manuscripts currently out will be accepted for publication. If one is, then I will know that you want me to go on writing." (Ahem! Here we have a flagrant abuse of putting out the fleece. Anger is not an appropriate reason.)

Bam! Bam! Bam! Within a week, all the manuscripts I had out were returned, and all were accompanied by rejection slips. According to my fleece, I should have quit. I tried, but by this time writing was a part of my daily schedule. Cutting it out of my day was like cutting out breakfast. So I prayed again. (More sincerely this time!) "God, have I misinterpreted? Have I misunderstood your call? What do you want me to do?"

During the next few days, God's presence was very real to me. It was as if he were physically present with me, with his hand on my shoulder, patting it, consoling me in much the same way a father might pat the shoulder of his child. As I worked around the house, feeling his touch, I could hear him saying to me, "You've done well. You've done right." Over and over, like a chorus, the words repeated themselves.

It was the kind of experience others might question, but for me it was what I needed to carry on. At least two more years passed before I gained any success as a writer. Often in moments of discouragement, in my memory, I would go back again to that time when I could feel God's hand on my shoulder and hear those words, "You've done well. You've done right." In response to my heartfelt prayer, God gave me a supernatural confirmation that I was on the right track—a confirmation that helped at the moment and continues to help me.

There are parts of the path of our earthly pilgrimage full of thorns and leading up steep declivities; parts of the way are overshadowed by clouds reaching down into the very valley of the shadow of death. Sometimes we are called upon to bear things that are almost unbearable, and to do things, in the weakness of the flesh, almost impossible; sometimes we sorely hunger for the viands of the heavenly banquet, and crave with intense longing the joys of everlasting and final deliverance.[3]

It is not wrong to pray for confirmation of God's will. It is not wrong at such times to ask for a glimpse of glory. Though the Holy Spirit is given to us as a pledge of all God will ultimately bestow on us, we still sometimes need a partial glimpse, some transfiguration experience here on earth, to enable us to carry on.

So, then, brother, sister, when your burden becomes too heavy, when life's ways become too dark, when the heart is too sore, when you are ready to perish, it is not amiss to pray to God to open the heavens, and through a rift in the sky to shine down into your heart some of the light of the Glory World.[4]

In realizing the rightness of praying for the confirmation of God's will or for a glimpse of his glory, we are not trying to duplicate Christ's experience. His experience was for the beloved Son of God. We wouldn't want to detract from its uniqueness or strive for an experience like his.

What we are saying is that through prayer we can be transfigured in spirit. We can be changed and renewed when we ask for a confirmation of God's direction or a glimpse of his glory. God will answer appropriately, giving us the necessary impetus to carry on.

One word of caution is needed. Our glimpse of glory, our personal transfiguration, is not to be an end in itself. Sometimes the experience of transfiguration is so precious that we want to magnify the experience, like Peter did. Peter wished to stay upon the mountain of transfiguration. He wanted to prepare three booths, to linger there, and not come down again (Matt. 17:4; Mark 9:5; Luke 9:33). Peter wanted to prolong his great moment. He did not want to go down to the everyday world again. He wanted to remain forever in the sheen of glory.

Our glimpse of glory is to be a temporary support. It is to give us strength to walk in the direction that God has chosen for us. The reaction of Jesus was to go down the mountain and to enter again into life. Jesus' withdrawal to the mountaintop to pray was not for escape but for preparation. Experiencing the glory of God and receiving confirmation of his will did not prompt Jesus to remain withdrawn. It put him right back on the path he had been walking; only now he walked with an even more certain step.

Notes

1. J. W. Shepard, *The Christ of the Gospels* (Grand Rapids, Michigan: William B. Eerdmans Publishing Company, 1956), p. 308.
2. William Barclay, *The Mind of Jesus,* pp. 180-181.
3. B. H. Carroll, *Messages on Prayer,* p. 40.
4. Ibid., p. 41.

7 When Jesus Departed from Custom

"And it came to pass, that, as he was praying in a certain place, when he ceased, one of his disciples said unto him, Lord, teach us to pray, as John also taught his disciples" (Luke 11:1). What was Jesus praying for in that "certain place"?

B. H. Carroll believes Jesus was praying that his disciples would want to learn to pray. He is inferring this on the basis of what happened immediately following the prayer. Because the disciples wanted to learn and because one of them asked, Carroll believes that is what Jesus was praying for. While we have accepted other inferred prayers in this book, this one is harder to accept. Why didn't Jesus tell the disciples what he wanted them to know about prayer? Why would Jesus pray for something he could obviously handle? Here's where we need more evidence. Let's look at some not-so-obvious evidence, that is, what the disciples already knew about prayer and the answer Jesus gave them.

The disciples already knew how to pray. The request suggests this. Their spokesman said, "Teach us to pray, as John also taught his disciples" (Luke 11:1). John the Baptist and some of the rabbis taught their followers an identifying kind of prayer. The prayer was to be repeated and distinguished them as a group. Now Jesus' followers were saying, "We want one, too."

The disciples were accustomed to praying. Their culture was immersed in prayer. There were morning prayers and evening prayers. Prayers were offered at nine, twelve, three, and before meals. There were prayers for every occasion. In fact, William Barclay says that no nation ever had a higher ideal of prayer and no religion ever ranked prayer higher in the scale of priorities than the Jews did.

But, as beautiful as these ideals were, faults crept in. The words fell glibly from their lips. The prayers for the special occasions were observed without meaning. There was a tendency toward long prayers, as if men battered long enough at God's door, he would answer. They believed God could be talked and even pestered into concessions. Knowing these things about the prayer life of the disciples makes Jesus' answer to their request very significant. His answer consisted of three parts—a prayer, a story, and an analogy.

The prayer Jesus gave the disciples is what we now call the Lord's Prayer or the Model Prayer (Luke 11:2-4). The Lord's Prayer is so familiar to us that it is hard for us to see what a break from tradition it was. Joachim Jeremias says this prayer was revolutionary in nature because it was an Aramaic prayer. The prayers the disciples already knew were in Hebrew, which was not their everyday language. Aramaic was. Jesus removed prayer from the liturgical sphere of sacred language and placed it right in the middle of everyday life.

The disciples had watched Jesus pray; they had heard him pray. They knew he talked to God as naturally, as intimately, and with the same sense of security as a child talks to his father. Jesus called God *Abba,* the Aramaic address of a small child for his father. No Jew would have dared to address God in this manner. With the Lord's Prayer, Jesus was saying to the disciples that they could do the same.

Next, Jesus told the disciples a story to emphasize how much God wants us to ask (Luke 11:5-10). It was a peculiar story about a man who tried to borrow bread in the middle of the night to serve a guest who had come in unexpectedly. The man wasn't ashamed to disturb his neighbor's sleep and to keep on asking until his neighbor gave him the bread he needed. Jesus' point was, Ask and persist in asking, like that man who needed bread.

But Jesus was careful not to liken God to the unwilling neighbor. As he went on talking he gave an analogy, likening God to a father (11:11-13). Jesus said that an earthly father will not give something that is forbidden or something with hidden danger in it in answer to a son's request. If an earthly father would not do that, would God? What God will give is himself, Jesus reassured (Luke 11:13).

Why did Jesus teach these three things to the disciples when all they wanted was a simple prayer to repeat? Jesus knew that with their current way of praying, according to the dictates of custom, they had lost the meaning of prayer. Jesus knew that when one prays mechanically, the reality of God is lost. If the disciples were going to follow him to the cross, if they were going to survive without him, they needed to grasp the reality of the One to whom they were praying. To do this, Jesus said, in effect, Use your natural conversational language when you pray. Talk to God with the same trust and intimacy that a child speaks to his daddy. Ask and keep on asking; God wants to hear from you. And once you have prayed this way, you will receive God himself. You will know for a certainty that he is real.

We can understand how exciting Jesus' answer was, how needful it was, and what a departure from custom it was. What we still do not understand is why Jesus would need to pray that the disciples would desire to learn to pray. Why didn't he just tell them what he wanted them to know?

Jesus did tell the disciples some of these things at other times (see Matt. 6:9-13; Matt. 7:7-11). Somehow those things weren't enough for a change. Jesus longed for a hunger, an interest on their part for his teachings on prayer to be effective, to really make a difference in their prayer lives. Their asking would indicate they were ready for this new kind of praying.

The disciples' asking would also indicate a willingness to receive. That willingness is important if real learning is to take place. Teachers have to spend a lot of valuable time motivating students to learn. How thrilling for the teacher when a student asks a significant question. With the attention of the student, the teacher can proceed to teach what all along he wanted to teach but couldn't because of the lack of willingness to learn.

The disciples' willingness to learn was most important because what Jesus was going to teach was such a departure from all they knew. Not until years later did the disciples fully realize the significance of what Jesus had said. Old ways and old customs die hard. For that reason, Jesus couldn't effectively introduce a new way of praying until the disciples indicated a readiness to learn.

While we can never be absolutely sure Jesus prayed that his disciples would desire to learn to pray, we can still benefit from this study. It shows we can't force what we believe on others, even when it may be for their own good. They simply will not receive our message until there is a hunger for it. Instead, we can do what Jesus did.

(1) Jesus gave the disciples the example of what real prayer is like. He prayed in their presence. On one occasion, Jesus was alone in prayer, yet in the presence of his disciples. We have discussed the spontaneity of his thanksgiving in the presence of his followers and others. The disciples saw what prayer did for Jesus and were intrigued.

(2) Jesus prayed for them to have a desire to learn to pray. We can pray for those we long to share salvation or

some spiritual truth with to have a desire to learn. In *Prayer: Conversing with God,* Rosalind Rinker writes about being concerned over the praying of a young college girl. The girl was completely unaware of the name she was using to address God when she prayed; she was using his name as a punctuation mark and not as though she was speaking to a real, living person. Rinker wanted to help her, but she couldn't afford to tell the girl what was wrong with her praying. So Rosalind prayed, "Lord, if you want me to speak with Marion and give her a few pointers, put it into her heart to come and see me."[1] That very night Marion knocked on Rosalind's door. Marion was ready to receive what Rosalind had to offer.

While we are living and praying for those we wish to help to show an interest, we can make certain that what happened to the disciples and other Jews of that day doesn't happen to us. For while we can never be sure Jesus was praying that his disciples might desire to learn to pray, we can be sure of Jesus' answer.

Those of us who are members of churches which do not observe a formal liturgy sometimes think we are immune from rote praying. As long as we don't repeat the Lord's Prayer in unison every Sunday, we feel like we have escaped what happened to the disciples. We have "real" praying, we assure ourselves; those in more formal churches only repeat words and go through motions. But that's not true. Prayer for any of us can become mechanical and habitual and without meaning once we lose our alertness. Then we lose our closeness with God, the closeness that is so vital if we are to face the unchangeable certainties in our lives.

We can keep our prayers from becoming mere words and exercises by remembering what Jesus told the disciples.

1. Pray using your normal conversational language—

the language which comfortably expresses your feelings and needs.

2. Ask and keep on asking. God wants to hear from you.

3. Talk to God with the same trust and intimacy a child feels when speaking to his daddy.

Do we have to put that much effort into our praying? Yes, we do because the underlying message of Jesus' answer is: Offer the real you to the real God. It keeps us from going into neutral when we pray. For the disciples, Jesus' answer represented a departure from custom. For us, it's a departure from routine.

Notes

1. Rosalind Rinker, *Prayer: Conversing with God* (Grand Rapids, Michigan: Zondervan Publishing House, 1959), p. 25.

8   When Praying Turns Tension Toward Triumph

When we look at the great people in history, we see them with their minds made up and their courses set. We see their hardened determination as they moved from triumph to triumph. We do not see their hesitations and uncertainties. We do not know the mental struggles through which they passed in secret before they saw their way and gained the necessary insight and courage to act.

We are guilty of doing the same thing when we look at Jesus. From where we stand, Jesus' triumph is so certain that it looks effortless and without strain. His courage is so calm, so sure, so seemingly inevitable, that it almost looks automatic. "So that we might very well dismiss it as no doubt glorious, but as largely meaningless for us. For he is he, and we are only we; and between us there is a great gulf fixed."[1]

We often think Jesus escaped things like tension, pressure, mental struggle, and emotional drain. Because he was the Son of God, with all of the resources of heaven on his side, he must have been immune from day-to-day stress. What we have seen so far of his prayer life has shown us otherwise. We'll see further evidence of the stress Jesus experienced as he approached the cross. In particular, we'll see it in John 12, where Jesus prayed a short prayer, "Father, glorify thy name." But before he prayed, he made a very significant statement, "Now is my soul troubled" (12:27). We only have to walk with him through the few events preceding this statement to understand the tension which produced it.

The Jewish authorities made plans to kill Jesus after he raised Lazarus from the grave (John 11:53). As the time for the Passover approached, Jesus became a much-talked-about, hunted man (John 11:56-57).

To avoid capture, Jesus withdrew to the desert for awhile. Then, six days before the Passover, he courageously approached Jerusalem (John 12:1). He went to Lazarus' home in Bethany near Jerusalem. Martha served him a meal, and Mary washed his feet with expensive perfume (John 12:3). When Judas protested the waste of the perfume, Jesus silenced him by saying that money could be given to the poor at any time but a kindness done to him *must be done now,* for soon the chance would never come again (John 12:7-8).

A large number of people came to Bethany to see Jesus. They also wanted to see Lazarus. So the chief priests made plans to kill not only Jesus but also Lazarus (John 12:11). This added pressure on Jesus complicated the situation even more.

The next day Jesus entered Jerusalem in such a way that every eye focused upon him. Many people were in Jerusalem for the Passover. They took branches of palm trees and went out to meet him, receiving him like the conqueror they wanted him to be. Very dramatically, Jesus chose to ride in on a donkey, a symbol that he was, indeed, the Messiah and that he was coming in peace. No one saw it that way, not even the disciples, causing more frustration for Jesus. The excitement surrounding Jesus' entry into Jerusalem infuriated the Jewish authorities even more. They became more determined than ever to kill Jesus.

Greeks were also in Jerusalem for the Passover. They

wanted to be a part of this crowd, and they wanted to meet Jesus. Philip and Andrew told Jesus some Greeks wanted to see him. The request of the Greeks was a sign to Jesus that his hour had come (John 12:23). The time was here to break down the wall that separated the Jews and the Gentiles.

Obviously, these emotionally-charged events were leading to a crisis. But Jesus' idea of what that crisis involved was quite different from anyone else's. When Jesus said, "The hour is come, that the Son of man should be glorified" (John 12:23), he meant he would be crucified on a cross. He didn't mean he would be a military conqueror who would subject the kingdoms of the world under his feet. He underscored his statement by saying that only by death comes life, only by spending life do we retain it, and only by service comes greatness.

It is one matter to say these things; it is another to be the life that gives itself, to be the seed that dies in the ground. "It was easy for Jesus to realize that the vocation of a seed is to die so that the fruit hidden within it may multiply . . . but much harder for him to accept the same vocation at the hands of his countrymen."[2]

Surely, this must have been a moment when Jesus wanted to withdraw from the crowd, to be alone. But by now, he was a curiosity attraction, a phenomenal miracle-worker. Among the hundreds of people gathered in Jerusalem for the Passover, he was the center of attention. The events from Bethany onward involved Jesus in emotional situations, from the expressed love pointing toward his burial to mob hysteria to the excitement of what the future would bring beyond the cross. The tension of it all gathered and hovered around him.

What did Jesus do? How did he respond to the emotional build-up? Not being able to escape the crowd, he more or less thought out loud. He expressed his tension,

"Now is my soul troubled . . . " (John 12:27). As soon as he did, he rejected his feelings as being totally inconsistent with his life and mission. "And what shall I say? Father, save me from this hour: but for this cause came I unto this hour" (John 12:27). He acknowledged his state of being and the certainty of his suffering. And then one big burst of prayer came forth, "Father, glorify thy name!" (John 12:28). It was a short, simple, honest prayer; but it was enough to turn the tide of his emotions from tension to triumph.

Immediately a voice from heaven was heard. "I have both glorified it, and will glorify it again" (John 12:28). God had been glorified by the work of Jesus in the past, and he would be glorified in the future. The crowd standing around heard the voice but were unable to distinguish what was said. Some said it was thunder, while others said an angel spoke to Jesus.

The voice, Jesus said, was for the people (John 12:30); the prayer was for Jesus. "Fortified by an overwhelming sense of heavenly approval, Jesus triumphantly cried, Now . . . is the judgement of this world."[3] Confidently he told them, "When I am lifted up from the earth, I will draw everyone to me" (John 12:32, TEV). The relief gained from the prayer served to steel Jesus' determination to go to the cross. He was certain that if he went on something would happen which would break the power of evil once and for all. If he was obedient to the cross, he was certain that a death blow would be struck to Satan, the ruler of this world. It was to be one last struggle which would break the power of evil forever. Further, he was certain that if he went to the cross, the sign of his upraised and crucified figure would, in the end, draw all men unto him.

What came between the tension and the triumph? What changed the one into the other? Jesus prayed on the spot, admitting his true feelings; he listened for God's answer; and he did not expect the tension to be totally removed. By his example, he gave us three good pointers for handling tension in our life.

1. *We must make ourselves pray.* No matter how dedicated the life, tension will gather. As long as we are involved with people, we are going to experience tension. Excitement, mental activity, pressure, stretching oneself too thin—all of these things can cause tension. Tension can build up so much that we begin to doubt whether prayer can even help. At those times, when we are doubting the value of prayer, we must *make* ourselves pray. Sometimes, merely praying aloud will break the tension.

The longer we put off praying, the harder it will be. To keep thinking, "One of these mornings, I'm going to get up early and pray this through" will not help. Whatever kind of prayer we can muster and say on the spot may be enough to break the tension. We can work through the underlying reasons for our tension later, during a time of withdrawal. Jesus did not wait for more appropriate surroundings. Right in the middle of people who did not fully understand him and, therefore, were not sympathetic to his needs, he uttered a prayer.

2. *We must be willing to listen for God's answer.* When Jesus prayed, the voice of God came to him. If you recall, the voice of God came to Jesus at his baptism when he first set out upon the work God had given him to do (Mark 1:11). It came to him on the mount of transfiguration when he finally decided to take the way which led to Jerusalem and to the cross (Mark 9:7). And then it came to him when he needed to be strengthened for the cross.

The incident here shows us two responses to God's voice: the response of the crowd and the response of Jesus. Jesus told the crowd the voice was for their sake, not his. Yet, as dramatic as a voice from heaven might be, it made no significant change in the people at the time. They went right on misunderstanding (John 12:34). Jesus was the one who was helped by the experience.

Could this comparison tell us something about listening to the voice of God? It takes a willing heart to really hear God's voice. Often in his ministry, Jesus would say, "Listen, then, if you have ears to hear." A spiritual sensitivity is necessary to receive God's direction; it's listening ears that belong to a willing heart. If we want to hear God's voice as clearly as Jesus did, then we must listen for it.

God is not a silent God, and ever and again, when the strain of life is too much for us, when the effort of God's way is beyond our human resources, if we listen we will hear Him speak, and we will go on with His voice ringing in our ears, and His strength surging through our frame. Our trouble is, not that God does not speak, but that we do not listen enough.[4]

3. *We must not always expect a final solution.* We must make ourselves pray in times of tension, and we need to listen for God's answer. What we must not do is expect a final solution to our tension *if* that tension is being caused by our faithfulness to God's will. The main source of Jesus' tension, his mission and the cross, were not removed from him by this prayer. Tension was temporarily relieved, thus enabling Jesus to go on; but there was more tension as he got nearer the cross.

Some kinds of tension can be removed once and for all with prayer; but there is also tension that is ongoing with God's will. This second kind of tension can be relieved, but we can't fully escape it until we are able to accomplish what God has called us to do.

Does experiencing this kind of tension make us less Christian? No. For it seems to be a built-in part of the Christian life, as we attempt to be righteous in an unrighteous world. The Christian life is not one that can be characterized as smooth-sailing. For years, I thought it ought to be. When someone said, "Wait on the Lord," I thought of a placid state of quietly, confidently, and unemotionally waiting for God to act. Certainly, it did not include outward or inner struggle.

While doing research for this book, I ran across a technical study on the Hebrew words that have been interpreted as "waiting on the Lord" in the Old Testament. The word study did not reveal the state of placidity I had pictured. According to the study, "waiting on the Lord" does call for quietness of humility and simplicity; it also revealed that tension was very much a part of the waiting. The author of the study says the man who waits in prayer will be "on the stretch for God." I liked that phrase because it more aptly describes what I had felt rather than the state of placidity I thought "waiting on the Lord" ought to be. Actually, my inability to ever achieve this state in thirty years of being a Christian should have been a clue that something was wrong with my thinking!

Being a committed Christian is to be involved in spiritual warfare (Eph. 6:10-13). As long as we have two opposing forces battling for our allegiance, we will experience tension. We should not condemn ourselves for experiencing it. We should acknowledge and face it honestly by making ourselves pray, by listening for God's answer, and by not always expecting a final solution for our tension. When we do these three things, we'll be able to turn our tension toward triumph as Jesus did. We'll be able to bridge that great gulf between ourselves and Jesus by realizing that he was in all points tempted as we are (Heb. 4:15).

Notes

1. *The Interpreter's Bible,* Vol. 8 (Nashville, Tennessee: Abingdon Press, 1955), pp. 664-665.

2. *The Broadman Bible Commentary,* Vol. 9, Luke-John, p. 322.

3. Ibid.

4. William Barclay, *The Gospel of John,* Vol. 2, Revised (Edinburgh, Scotland: The Saint Andrew Press, 1975), p. 148.

9   When Jesus Prayed for an Apostle

Some Christians believe that each thing that happens in this life is related to faith. If we could somehow manage enough impeccable faith, we could rise above all the strife, stress, and temptations that this life offers. This belief places a heavy responsibility on the shoulders of Christians. Then, when difficulties enter our lives, it is because we failed, because we did not have the kind of faith we should. But one of the intercessory prayers made by Jesus just may show that this is not altogether accurate thinking.

The Bible does not record the exact words of this prayer. It is a prayer Jesus said he had prayed. The Last Supper was over. The disciples had just quarreled over who would be the greatest. Jesus declared his knowledge of a traitor in their midst and then mentioned a prayer that he *had* prayed.

" 'Simon, Simon! Listen! Satan has received permission to test all of you, to separate the good from the bad, as a farmer separates the wheat from the chaff. But I have prayed for you, Simon, that your faith will not fail. And when you turn back to me, you must strengthen your brothers' " (Luke 22:31-32, TEV).

Talking to Peter, the leader of the disciples, Jesus cautioned about the hours immediately ahead. The events would test the disciples' faith. The whole group faced testing which could not be avoided and for which none of them were adequately prepared.

This time of testing was coming by divine permission. Jesus said that Satan had received permission to test them. Jesus' words remind us of the beginning of the book of Job. In that Old Testament story, Satan requested permission from God to test the faith of Job. That Satan requested permission from God teaches us that evil is not ultimate in the universe. Satan does have power in the lives of men, but his power is limited.

Jesus used the picture of the farmer separating the grain from the chaff to describe what the days ahead would be like for the disciples. Sifting the grain is the last step in cleaning grain of chaff and other impurities. One writer said, "Violent shaking in a sieve makes this process a fitting description of the agitation that tries one's faith almost to the point of destroying it." The future would be turbulent for the disciples and specifically for Peter.

We are not to think that Jesus did not pray for all the disciples, but he singled out Peter who was in special danger and in dire need of his help. Jesus' prayer was not that Satan should be prohibited from testing Peter, but rather that his faith wouldn't fail.

Jesus described his act of praying as earnestly asking on behalf of Peter. Jesus did not pray that Peter would not be tested by Satan. Rather he prayed that Peter would not utterly collapse while being tested. In this way, Jesus expressed his confidence in Peter, as well as his concern for him.

Jesus did not ask that Peter be freed from trouble. Undergoing difficulties and hardships is an integral part of the Christian way. The quality of Peter's faith in such circumstances was important, and he was given the assurance of mighty intercession on his behalf.

Considering Jesus' mighty intercession for Peter, strange events followed—strange because it looked like Peter's faith did fail. Peter proclaimed absolute loyalty to Jesus (Luke 22:33). Peter said he was "ready to go to prison" and "to die" with Jesus. No greater statement of commitment could have been made. Peter may have expected Jesus to have commended him for his loyalty. Instead, Peter heard a sober prediction. "I tell you, Peter," Jesus said, "the rooster will not crow tonight until you have said three times that you do not know me" (Luke 22:34, TEV). The record that follows (Luke 22:54-60) shows Peter doing exactly what Jesus predicted. Because Peter denied Jesus, does that mean Peter's faith failed? And, if his faith failed, does that mean Jesus' prayer for Peter wasn't answered?

Judging from the events that follow the prayer, it does look like Peter's faith failed. Obviously, Peter was disloyal after Jesus prayed. We have to accept that fact; accepting that Jesus' prayer was not answered yes is hard for some of us. Surely, if anyone received whatever he asked for in prayer, wouldn't Jesus be the one?

There are some who think not. They have no problem with looking at this as a prayer that was prayed sincerely and confidently, but nevertheless was not answered yes. No question about it—it is a no answer to prayer.

Others try to make a yes answer out of Peter's experience. One Bible expositor said that Peter's faith did not fail; his hope did. He said Peter's faith did not fail when he was denying Jesus; neither did his love fail. What failed was his hope and, therefore, his courage. Peter's hope was dead. When hope is gone, courage fails, and cowardice sets in.

While it is true that courage fails in the absence of hope, I believe this explanation is looking at Peter's situation a little unrealistically. It almost looks like the expositor is trying to read a yes into a no situation, as if he cannot possibly accept the fact that Jesus might have received a no answer to such earnest praying.

There is a more realistic way of looking at the situation than either a yes or no answer. Failure there would be, but not utter failure. Jesus seemed to know exactly what would happen. While he was certain of Peter's denial, he was also confident in his prayer and in Peter. Jesus' words indicate this: " 'But I have prayed for you, Simon . . . . And when you turn back to me, you must strengthen your brothers" (Luke 22:32, TEV).

"But I . . . " makes the difference. Satan might have been granted power to sift the disciples, but Jesus was confident that Satan would gain only temporary victory. Why was Jesus so certain of this? Because he had prayed. Jesus would not be discouraged by a momentary lapse of Peter's faith or despondent because of his denials. Jesus' prayer would hold Peter.

Notice the confidence Jesus expressed. He said, "*When* you turn back . . . " not "*if* you turn back." "Turn back" means to reaffirm loyalty or retrace your steps. Jesus knew Peter was no calculating deserter; he wasn't planning denial. Peter's loyalty to Jesus would lapse temporarily, but it would return. Jesus was confident of the ultimate issue. Jesus knew Peter was a man of limited foresight and uncertain responses, and he knew he would return.

Then Jesus said a lovely thing to Peter: "Strengthen your brothers." The others, too, would be denying Jesus only in a not so obvious way. They were sharing in the sifting ordeal and would fail too. They would need someone to help them reestablish their faith and their sense of direction and purpose. It was as if Jesus were saying to Peter,

"You will deny me, but the result will be that you will be able to help your brothers who are going through the sifting too."

Jesus dealt with Peter frankly and prophetically that the other disciples might benefit. Satan would pass Peter through a sieve of temptations; but because of the intercession of Jesus, the chaff would be separated from the wheat. Peter would deny Jesus but he would repent and come back a humbler and wiser man.

From the beginning of his ministry, Jesus had seen possibilities in Peter that no one else had seen. Jesus had seen the qualities that would equip Peter for dedicated discipleship and a unique leadership role among the early Christians. To Peter Jesus said, "I will give unto thee the keys of the kingdom" (Matt. 16:19). Later Peter became a great undershepherd of the Lord's flock. He followed Jesus to prison and to a martyr's death on a cross, as he said he would, but not until his faith had been tested.

The way God answered Jesus' prayer should help us understand some of the answers we receive to our prayers. When we pray for some "thing," it is easy to gauge when the answer comes. The answers are not so easy to discern when we are praying for a work of grace in our lives or in the life of someone else. The answer may not come in completed form, but may well come in the form of a process as it did with Peter. When praying for Peter's faith not to fail, Jesus was not asking that Peter be able to meet all of life with a blazing faith, never faltering and never doubting. The answer came as a process. When the process was completed, Peter's faith was strong and healthy.

There's sort of an unwritten theology hovering among pray-ers that if we pray for something and God does answer, the answer should be in exactly the form we want. We think no problems or struggles should be connected with answers to prayer, but this prayer in the life of Jesus shows us that is not true.

We must face honestly the paradox that, although we expect all prayers to be answered simply and directly, they are not always. Not even all of Jesus' prayers were answered simply and directly. Many of us isolate Jesus' teachings on prayer without looking at his prayer life. We assume that if we pray hard enough, we will get what we want. Such statements as Jesus made in Mark 9:23; Matthew 17:20; 21:22; and Mark 11:24 indicate this, but his prayer life shows us otherwise as we have seen and will continue to see as he draws nearer the cross.

Seeing that the answers to Jesus' prayers were not always what we would expect them to be should help keep us from being disillusioned and shattered when similar answers occur in response to our own prayers. The answer may come in the form of a process, as it did with Peter. Something more beautiful and stronger than we had hoped for might be produced in our lives.

We should also remember that along with this process goes the assurance of Jesus' intercession for us. What Jesus did for Peter, he does for us. Jesus continually intercedes for us (see Rom. 8:34; Heb. 7:25; and 1 John 2:1).

When Jesus left earth and ascended to the Father, he did not stop praying. He still prays. Jesus is a "priest for ever" (Heb. 7:17), and he "continueth ever," having "an unchangeable priesthood" (Heb. 7:24). Therefore, there is never a single moment when his prayers on our behalf do not reach our heavenly Father. Jesus exercises the priestly function of his office without interruption or interference. B. H. Carroll summarized it well: " . . . but for the intercession of Jesus there would not necessarily be perpetuity in our faith; that it is his love for us that prevents us from turning him loose altogether in the hour of trial."[1]

Jesus as our continual intercessor is a hard concept for us to grasp and understand. How Jesus could intercede for every believer is mind-boggling. His intercession is not necessarily expressed in words. Neither is it a continual offering of himself to God. Neither is his being before the throne a ceaseless reminder to the Father that Jesus died for us.

That Jesus Christ prays for us in an impressive thought; and it becomes doubly impressive when we recall that he intercedes for us as the Lord of Glory. Not with strong crying and tears does he intercede for us now, but with kingly sovereignty that is divine and all-prevailing.[2]

While we may never understand how Jesus intercedes for us, we can believe it and count on it. When we do that, the intercession of Jesus will become a great comfort to us. It will teach us to rest more and more in the love of this unseen, but ever-present, Friend. It will anchor our souls.

In more practical terms, Jesus' intercession means we do not hold the rope of faith alone. When we cannot walk in faith any longer, Jesus' prayers carry us through.

The first time I experienced this cooperative holding of the rope of faith was when my husband was trying to get a job following his graduate school days. Bob was in the field of higher education—a field highly saturated with applicants. From the minute Bob began graduate school, I began praying a job would be available for him when he finished.

In January of the year Bob was to graduate in May, he began sending his placement papers to various colleges. In agreement (Matt. 18:19), we prayed that he would have a job by graduation.

Graduation came and went with no job, not even an interview, in sight.

The job Bob held during graduate school was scheduled

to end at the end of June. We prayed that he would have a job by the end of June. June 30 came with no job, no interviews, and now, no means of support.

Then we prayed for Bob to get a position in time for us to move before school started because of our children. During July, Bob did have some interviews, but time for school enrollment came with no job in sight. The opening of school for our children also meant that colleges were ready to open with full staffs; from this point on, very few would be hiring.

The day I enrolled our children in school, I stopped believing Bob was going to get a job in higher education. God had not responded to two years of faith-believing, specifically asking prayers. Weary of asking, I simply quit.

I was surprised to learn how dismal life is when we don't believe God will act. For about two weeks, I was morbid until I couldn't stand myself any longer. "All right, Lord," I prayed, "I'm going to work at believing in you. I'm going to trust you to work out this situation. How about a job for Bob by September 1?"

By September 1, Bob did have a job. (We received the good news on August 29!) When he got the job, one of my friends said to me, "Now, aren't you ashamed of the way you acted? Aren't you ashamed that you stopped believing?"

"No, I'm not," I responded. "It wasn't something I did deliberately. I couldn't help myself. I had asked all I could ask."

Actually, my response was one of marvel at God's faithfulness. The job Bob got was one he had interviewed for back in July. The marvel to me was that God hadn't withdrawn the job when my faith faltered. His reaction wasn't, "I had a nice job for Bob but Brenda stopped believing. Consequently, I'll have to withdraw the job."

The reason God didn't withdraw the job was Jesus' intercession. Jesus held the rope of faith when I could no longer hold it. His prayers secured Bob's job, and I have been made stronger because of his help. Being a faith-believing Christian is no longer the heavy responsibility it once was. Like Peter, who discovered through experience that he was not alone, I also discovered that I am not alone. Jesus and I hold the rope of faith together.

Notes

1. B. H. Carroll, *Messages on Prayer*, p. 52.

2. James G. S. S. Thomson, *The Praying Christ* (Grand Rapids, Michigan: William B. Eerdmans Publishing Company, 1959), p. 118.

10 When Jesus Prays for the Holy Spirit

Jesus, in his last conversation with his followers, told them about a prayer he had already prayed. The Gospel writer John, in recording the last conversation, mentioned a prayer that Jesus was going to pray. Jesus said, "I will pray the Father, and he shall give you another Comforter" (John 14:16).

Obviously, when Jesus said "another," he was referring to someone like himself who would come in response to his prayer. Jesus called that someone, Comforter. Actually, Comforter is the King James Version of the name for the one who would come. The word in the Greek is *parakletos*. The word *parakletos* means someone who is called in. William Barclay says the reason the person is called in gives the word its distinctive associations. Here are some examples which Barclay lists in his *Daily Study Bible.*

A *parakletos* might be a person called in to give witness in a law court in someone's favor.

A *parakletos* might be an advocate called in to plead someone's cause when someone was under a charge which would issue in serious penalty.

A *parakletos* might be an expert called in to give advice in some difficult situation.

A *parakletos* might be a person called in to put new courage into the hearts and minds of a company of soldiers who were depressed and dispirited.

Always a *parakletos* is someone called in to help by a person in trouble, distress, doubt, or bewilderment.

If we put all of these ideas together, we have a good description of this person Jesus is going to pray for. When we do, we see that the word *Comforter,* which mostly has to do with sorrow in our way of thinking, doesn't begin to describe what a real *parakletos* is.

The person Jesus was praying for is much more than a comforter. He is the Holy Spirit. So what Jesus was saying in his last conversation with his followers was, "I am setting before you a hard task, and I am sending you out on an engagement that is going to be very difficult. But I am going to pray for someone, the Holy Spirit, who will guide you in what to do and who will enable you to do it."

By examining the word *parakletos,* we know who Jesus was praying for. What we don't know is when Jesus prayed this prayer or why he had to pray it.

The Bible does not tell us when Jesus prayed this prayer. Since Jesus made this reference the night of his arrest, perhaps he was going to pray that night. It is hard for us to see when the prayer could have been prayed then because the trial and crucifixion soon followed.

Some people believe this was not a prayer prayed during Jesus' life on earth, rather it is a prayer prayed at sometime in the believer's life. This view places strong emphasis on the conjunction *and* between verses 15 and 16. "If ye love me, keep my commandments. And I will pray the Father, and he shall give you another Comforter" (John 14:15-16). In other words, as we grow in our love for Jesus, he will, in turn, pray to the Father to give us more of the Holy Spirit.

Most scholars, however, believe this prayer was said sometime between the last conversation Jesus had with his disciples and Pentecost. Pentecost is a festival observed yearly by the Jews, but to Christians the word means one thing—the coming of the Holy Spirit, as recorded in Acts 2.

When we say the Holy Spirit came at Pentecost, we do not mean he was absent from the world before that date. The Holy Spirit was from the beginning. The power and the action of the Holy Spirit were connected with extraordinary and abnormal happenings in the Old Testament. The great utterances and the great visions of the prophets and sudden manifestations of the splendor of God were the work of the Holy Spirit. But in the New Testament, after Pentecost, the Holy Spirit became the moving, controlling, and upholding power for everyday life and everyday action.

The Holy Spirit came at Pentecost to indwell all believers. In the Old Testament, this indwelling of the Spirit was not for all the people of the Lord. It was a special privilege; it was a gift bestowed upon a special few for special purposes. The Spirit of God came upon a select few at certain seasons (Judg. 13:25). But in the new day, after Pentecost, the gift was not just for a Samson, a Samuel, or a Saul. The Spirit is for all who believe in the Lord.

One seminary professor characterized what happened at Pentecost in this way. He said the Holy Spirit entered history in a normative way at Pentecost; therefore, Pentecost is to the Holy Spirit what Bethlehem is to Jesus.

Because Pentecost is such a pivotal point in the work of the Holy Spirit, we say the Spirit came at Pentecost. We believe that is what Jesus had in mind when he prayed for the Holy Spirit to come. Therefore, we reason, the prayer must have been prayed sometime between the last conversation with his followers and Pentecost.

In addition to not knowing when the prayer was prayed, we don't know why Jesus needed to pray for the coming of the Holy Spirit. Why was Jesus' prayer necessary?

Certainly, the prayer wasn't necessary to convince God. The coming of the Holy Spirit had already been fore-ordained (Joel 2:28-32); God, the Father, didn't need to be pressed into giving the Holy Spirit.

Perhaps prayer was needed because the coming of the Holy Spirit involved the will of Jesus. Prayer is the way of giving our wills over to God to do with, in, and through us what he would like to do. We have a personal relationship with him, so he does not treat us as inanimate objects—as blocks of wood ready to be hammered, sawed, and painted into his likeness. By choice, we offer our wills to him. We do this by praying, more specifically by asking.

This kind of reasoning may be too simplistic with regard to the necessity of Jesus' prayer. Yet we have much evidence that shows how much Jesus' will was involved in the coming of the Holy Spirit. From what Jesus said and from what he did, clearly his will was involved in the coming of the Holy Spirit.

Jesus let his followers know the Holy Spirit was coming and that he would have a part in the Holy Spirit's coming (John 7:38-39; John 14:16,17,26; John 15:26; John 16:7,12,13; Luke 24:49; and Acts 1:4-5). Jesus referred to the Holy Spirit as the one whom the Father will send in his name (John 14:26). He also said the Holy Spirit was the one "whom I will send unto you from the Father" (John 15:26). And "It is expedient for you that I go away: for if I go not away, the Comforter will not come unto you; but if I depart, I will send him unto you" (John 16:7). When Jesus bodily left this world, he promised to send the Holy Spirit to his people. His promise involved his will.

There would not have been a Holy Spirit in the Pente-costal sense that we know him without the life, death, burial, resurrection, and ascension of Jesus. Whether an actual, verbal prayer was said, Jesus' suffering and death became prayers to make way for the coming of the Holy Spirit.

The prayer for the Holy Spirit was not to convince the Father. Because of the prayer the Son was able to give his will over to the Father, not an easy thing to do in light of the cross.

While we have wondered about the when and the why of this prayer, we do not have to wonder about whether it was answered. We not only have the biblical evidence of Pentecost (Acts 2) but also we have other evidence that this prayer was answered. The evidence is within Christians through the possession of the Holy Spirit.

Some Christians believe that if there has been a release of certain of the gifts of the Holy Spirit (Rom. 12:6-8, 1 Cor. 12:8-10; 28-30) and Eph. 4:11) in our lives, we possess the Holy Spirit. Others believe that we have the Holy Spirit in our lives if the fruits of the Spirit are developing and maturing (Gal. 5:22-23). These are valid, biblical tests, but the test I like best is what I call the Abba-Father test.

Paul said that when we are God's children, when we possess his Spirit, we'll cry out, "Abba, Father" (Rom. 8:15-16; Gal. 4:6). We have seen that *abba* is the loving term Jesus called God. It was a revolutionary departure from custom for Jesus to call God *abba* and for him to teach his disciples to do so. It showed that a relationship with God can be very close. When reporting this close relationship in Greek, the Gospel writers used the Aramaic *abba,* the very term Jesus used to express the wonderful relationship he had with God, rather than trying to translate it.

In other words, after Pentecost, Jesus' followers were able to have a close relationship with God because of the Holy Spirit. They felt God; they experienced him; they talked with him; and they followed him because of the Holy Spirit within them. They recognized that they were tapping in to the kind of relationship Jesus had with the Father, and they responded as Jesus did: "Abba, Father!"

To have an Abba-Father experience does not mean that we have to respond at some time in our lives with those exact words. The followers held those words as a precious memory of Jesus. It had been Jesus' way of showing his closeness, his vital relationship with the Father. When the Spirit moved within the followers, they recognized his presence and responded as Jesus did.

We may not respond to the Spirit's presence within us in the same ways. The words we say are not the test. The certainty of the Spirit within us is the test. We know when the Spirit resides within.

During the time I was writing this book, my husband was treated unjustly by some fellow Christians. Both of us were deeply hurt. In trying to survive the injustice, we found ourselves in the vulnerable position of continually being hurt. (What we also had to consider was that we may have collected a few extra hurts to make the injustice seem all the more greater!)

At the same time, I began noticing the amount of friction among Christians. Both the secular and religious presses seem to report a lot of it. One day the weight of the hurt and the confusion of the friction caved in on me, and I let the questions surface that had been circulating in my mind for weeks. *Why continue to be a Christian? Why keep at it? Why keep trying to do God's work? Why write another book on prayer?*

But as sure as these questions were in my mind, so was the reality of the presence of Jesus Christ. He is real. He has made and is making a difference in my life. Consequently, I can't help but respond. I can't help but go on. While I may never understand the behavior of Christians,

I do know the reality of Jesus Christ because of the Holy Spirit's presence within.

For me, the certainty is, "I can't help but write."

For Paul, it was, "Abba, Father."

For you, it may be, "Thank you, Jesus," or "I love you, Father."

The words are not important to the Abba-Father test, the certainty is. We may never be able to prove this kind of relationship to others; but when we have it, we know it.

The experience of God's Holy Spirit moving within us gives us absolute confirmation that he is real and gives us absolute confirmation that a prayer Jesus prayed at a time and place we know not has been answered. Jesus prayed to the Father, and the Holy Spirit has come. We know, because he lives within us. Hallelujah!

11 When Jesus Prayed with Startling Confidence

Jesus' reference to a prayer he was going to pray for the Holy Spirit took place in his farewell talks with his close followers. These talks, collected in John 14—17, contain some of the most beautiful and reassuring words Jesus ever spoke; they also include warnings of hard times and persecution. Obviously, Jesus' intent was one of preparation. Climax was near, and he knew time was short in which to conclude the preparation of those dearest and nearest to him. He ended his talk with a prayer (John 17). By praying, it is as if Jesus were saying, "I have done all I can do. I have said all I can say. Now I commit you and the future to the hands of God."

This prayer is the longest of Jesus' recorded prayers. It's too long to repeat here, so you might like to read it in your Bible before reading this chapter.

Because it is Jesus' longest, continuous prayer, many books have been written about it. Each line has been dissected and analyzed many times. Instead of doing another dissection, this will be an overall view of the prayer to see how it fits into the whole of Jesus' prayer life. What unique contribution does this prayer make? As a whole, what does this prayer teach us?

This prayer could teach us a lot about intercession, adding strength to the intercessory role we saw in chapter 9. The urgency with which Jesus expresses himself, probably due to the short time left, could also help us. The prayer could offer us some practical lessons in how to use God's name in praying. Even looking at the prayer as a whole, there are many lessons for us. But what stands out to me, what I continue to marvel about, is the confidence expressed in the prayer. Jesus' long prayer shows confidence in God and in his followers—a confidence that is almost incomprehensible considering the circumstances he was facing and considering who he had to work with.

Jesus was facing the cross. While all along he knew the cross would be there, "the hour," as he said in this prayer, "is come" (John 17:1). In three short years, he had finished the work God sent him to do. He had been faithful to the life and to the mission God had given him. "A little earlier the thousands had thronged to him . . . but now many of these no longer stood beside him in his hour of supreme trial . . . . Instead of bitterly resenting these heartbreaking results, Jesus rejoiced over his modest remnant as a manifestation of divine generosity."[1] With all the world shouting that he was a failure, with death staring him in the face, Jesus was grateful for those the Father had given him (John 17:6-8).

Jesus prayed for the close followers the Father had given him. He prayed that they would be one as he and the Father are one (John 17:11). It's hard to fathom Jesus' confidence in his close followers and their ability to be united. We have seen how vulnerable Peter was and how his faith was going to fail him. We have seen how the disciples often misinterpreted who Jesus was and what his mission was. Just before this prayer, at the Last Supper, they argued over who was going to be the greatest.

Confidence in the disciples was remarkable considering how hard it would be to achieve unity with such a group. It is even more remarkable when we note the enormous responsibility Jesus was going to give them. In the early days of the church, their task would be an awesome one. They would make the resurrection a living reality to the world. The authentic record of Jesus' words and deeds would come through the inspired writings of some of the followers.

Elton Trueblood says, "These men were very important for the whole world, because if they should fail, there was no other way of assuring the continuance of the redemptive leaven, without which the world could not rise. Though these, hopefully, would be followed by a host of future witnesses, for the time being the sole responsibility was upon them. For the moment, for this crucial 'hour,' they were the saving salt."[2] If they were to be the "saving salt," they would need protection (John 17:11), joy (John 17:13), preservation from the evil one (John 17:15), and sanctification (John 17:17). Jesus asked for these things for them.

The greatest portion of Jesus' prayer was offered in behalf of the disciples. His prayer was not a petition set against the Father's will for them. Rather, it is a consultation born of confident assurance that the Father and the Son shared the same purpose for these followers.

At that precise moment the disciples were few and weak. Very soon they would all flee and leave Jesus to face his enemies alone. Yet Jesus had confidence in the disciples. Though they did not understand—and would not for some days—he still risked his future work on their bewildered shoulders.

Gradually, Jesus' prayer broadened in scope. He looked beyond the men immediately around him. He looked through the coming centuries and saw in one comprehensive glance all those the Father was going to give him. He saw those of us who would be gathered to him through the message and ministry of the disciples (John 17:20). His request for us was like what he requested for the twelve; he asked for unity (John 17:21).

Unity is difficult even in a small group like that of the twelve who at this time were far from united. How much more difficult it is among millions of people scattered all over the earth.

The history of the early church, as reported in the New Testament, reveals that often the believers were far from united. The church was often threatened with division. In Jerusalem there was the deception of Ananias and Sapphira (Acts 5:1-11) and the quarrel over the care of Greek widows (Acts 6). As Christianity spread, other problems arose, such as disagreement between Paul and Barnabas over John Mark (Acts 15:36-41), the problems in Corinth, and the schism over the status of Gentile Christians.

The history of the church from New Testament times on shows us the same thing. Unity and Christianity have not gone hand in hand. One example of friction among believers in early Christendom was over whether the Holy Spirit proceeded from Jesus the Son or from God the Father. This issue is what caused the final split between the Eastern Church and the Western Church. The creed followed by these two groups did not expressly state that the Holy Spirit proceeded from the Son as well as the Father, but both groups generally believed that he did. But when an attempt was made to add "and the Son" to the creed, anger and division resulted. The argument between the two groups was over John 15:26 (". . . Spirit of truth, which proceedeth from the Father . . . "), and John 16:7 (" . . . if I depart, I will send him"). Both verses were part of Jesus' last conversation with his followers. They were part of the conversation which ended in Jesus' prayer for unity!

In light of what history shows us regarding the nature of

believers, how do we interpret Jesus' prayer for unity? Surely Jesus was not overconfident, knowing the nature of men the way he did? Or, was his prayer one that has gone unanswered? Is unity among Jesus' followers a dream that can never be fulfilled?

Elton Trueblood has a good answer. He says we should look at the answer to Jesus' prayer for unity for those of us who would come after the disciples as a process. He says, "What is important to know is that unity is something to be *achieved,* and that, like freedom, it can come only at the end of an arduous process and never at the beginning."[3] Trueblood quotes Ephesians 4:13 to add strength to his view. "And so we shall all come together to that oneness in our faith and in our knowledge of the Son of God; we shall become mature people, reaching to the very height of Christ's full stature" (TEV).

Someone else makes this explanation: "The kind of unity Jesus was talking about was a unity of personal relationship. It was the type of unity that ties a Paul of Tarsus, Luther of Germany, Wesley of England, and Moody of America together. Though these men were widely separated in time, space, nationality, education and church connections, they were one in the essentials of a common faith. Such unity was what Jesus petitioned in his prayer as the underlying spiritual unity which enabled his disciples to bear a convincing testimony before the world."

Either of these explanations shows that Jesus' prayers were not always answered in simple and direct ways we can understand. It also means that this particular prayer is still answered and that we are partially responsible for the answer. Are we contributing to the unity Jesus prayed for? If we become smug about a particular spiritual experience we've had or consider our revelation of God to be more accurate than others or if we think our denomination teaches the only way to heaven, we are in danger of hindering Jesus' prayer from being answered. Of course, we should be grounded in what we believe and have doctrinal convictions; but when we begin to think our way is the "inside" track, we are hindering the process of unity for which Jesus prayed.

Jesus knew that what had begun in him would continue far into the future. His vision included a long line of believers who would bear faithful witness, so there would be believers in each generation. The basic nature of the spiritual experience future believers would have would be identical with that of the first disciples. This spiritual experience is to unite us.

How could Jesus be so beautifully and strongly confident in the circumstances he was facing and considering who he had to work with? The prayer gives us two important clues: (1) faith in God and (2) faith in men.

In manner and word Jesus' prayer showed his faith in God. His manner of praying—his humility, the way he used God's name—indicate Jesus' close respect for and obedience to the Father and the trust Jesus had in God.

Jesus' words also reveal the close relationship between the Father and the Son. Jesus said they were together before the world was made (John 17:5). He asked that the followers be one just as he and God were one (John 17:11,22). He was anticipating going to the Father (John 17:13), and he said that God had loved him before the world was made (John 17:24). Their oneness was so complete that Jesus said, "I made you known to them, and I will continue to do so, in order that the love you have for me may be in them, and so that I also may be in them" (John 17:26, TEV).

In this prayer, Jesus made one of the greatest claims he ever made. He said, "All I have is yours, and all you have is mine . . . '' (John 17:10, TEV). The first part of that sentence is natural and easy to understand, for all things belong to God. But the second part, "All that you have is mine . . . '', is an astonishing claim. William Barclay says, "Never did Jesus so vividly lay down His kinship, His unity, His oneness with God. Jesus is so one with God that He exercises the very power and perogatives of God.''[4]

Herschel H. Hobbs says, "The greatest demonstration of his love is seen at Calvary. But the supreme essence of his oneness with the Father and with his followers is seen in this prayer.''[5] The essence of oneness with the Father is understandable, knowing the nature of the Father and of Jesus. But faith in his followers? Faith in men? Confidence in people like ourselves? Now that is incomprehensible!

Mankind is more naturally divided than united. It is more human to fly apart than to come together, yet Jesus had confidence in the disciples. He was with the men God had given him, and he thanked God for them. He never doubted that they would carry on the work he had planned for them to do. He had twelve Galilean peasants; they were enough for Jesus. From our way of viewing success, when Jesus left this world, there was not much hope for Christianity to succeed. He seemed to have achieved so little and to have won so few. The great, orthodox, religious people of the day turned against him, but Jesus was neither afraid nor pessimistic about the future. His attitude was, "I have only won twelve ordinary men; but with those twelve ordinary men, I will change the world.''

Jesus put his trust and confidence in men and in God, and we need to also. As Christians, we want to always be growing in our faith in God. That should be a priority in our lives, but we also need some confidence in people.

This is not to suggest an equal confidence in God and in people but that *both* are needed.

Every missionary must believe in people as well as in God. He must believe that some people wil respond to his message. She must believe that when the Holy Spirit works within the hearts of people as they hear the message she brings some will eventually respond.

Every preacher who begins a new work or who has a vision of accomplishing some task must believe that eventually someone is going to catch his vision or be willing to join him in the task. To believe otherwise is to wrap ourselves in pessimism and seriously limit the work of God.

Norman Vincent Peale is a person who has confidence in men and God. When hiring people to work for him, he chooses people not on the basis of their present spiritual conviction but on the basis of other qualities which he feels are important to the job. He does this in the confidence that if Christianity is the irresistible thing he claims it to be from the pulpit, then in time sheer contact will bring about conversion.[6] He believes in men and their ability to change, and he trusts God to bring about that change.

Jesus had that kind of confidence in people and in God. He chose twelve men out of the multitudes who heard him. He watched these men come to grips with discipleship. He knew that if these responded, others on down the line would too. Jesus looked confidently to these men to spread his name through the world. He knew they did not fully understand him. He knew that in a very short time they were going to abandon him in his hour of greatest need. Yet his confidence in them and in God was unshaken.

After this prayer Jesus was to face the betrayal, the trial, and the cross. He would not have any other conversation with his disciples before his death. It is a wonderful and precious thing to remember that his last words were not of despair but of confidence in God and in men.

Notes

1. *The Broadman Bible Commentary,* Vol. 9, p. 346.
2. Elton Trueblood, *The Lord's Prayers,* p. 100.
3. Ibid., p. 101.
4. William Barclay, *The Gospel of John,* Vol. 2, p. 251.
5. Herschel H. Hobbs, *Studying Adult Life and Work Lessons,* January-February-March, 1978 (Nashville, Tennessee: Convention Press, 1977), pp. 78-79.
6. John L. Sherrill, *Christian Life,* February 1970 (Wheaton, Illinois: Christian Life Publications, Inc.).

12 A Prayer of Intense Emotion

We leave a prayer of confidence to look at a prayer of intense, agonizing emotion that asked for escape. It's hard to believe the two prayers were said by the same person, just hours apart, but they were. After Jesus prayed his intercessory prayer of startling confidence, he went to the garden of Gethsemane (John 18:1). There, he prayed that if it were possible, he be spared the cup of suffering which lay ahead (Mark 14:32-42; Matt. 26:36-46; Luke 22:39-46).

Three times Jesus prayed that the cup be taken from him. Putting it that way makes it sound like short, pithy praying; but it was not. His disciples fell asleep while he was praying. They could hardly have had time to do that if the praying consisted only of what is recorded. What is recorded tells us the main thrust of what Jesus was seeking from the Father. He was seeking a way out as he struggled with God's will.

A casual reading of the Gethsemane experience reveals that this prayer was one of emotion. "And he taketh with him Peter and James and John, and began to be sore amazed, and to be very heavy; And saith unto them, My soul is exceeding sorrowful unto death: tarry ye here, and watch. And he went forward a little, and fell on the ground, and prayed that, if it were possible, the hour might pass from him" (Mark 14:33-35). As Jesus continued to pray, an angel appeared and strengthened him (Luke 22:43). Then he prayed even more fervently; his sweat was like drops of blood falling to the ground (Luke 22:44).

A deeper study, looking into the meaning of the words as they appeared in the original text of the New Testament, indicates just how intense the emotion was. Here are some of the things Curtis Mitchell explains in his book *Praying Jesus' Way*.

1. When Jesus had the other disciples wait while he took Peter, James, and John with him deeper into the garden, the Bible says he "began to be sorrowful and very heavy" (Matt. 26:37). Mitchell says, "The word *began* indicates the commencement of a new level of sorrow more severe in degree than our Lord had ever experienced before!"[1]

2. Jesus' emotional state is described as "sorrowful" by Matthew (26:37) and "sore amazed" by Mark (14:33). This carries the idea of sorrow to the point of great amazement. Mitchell says, "One could almost translate it by the word *terrified!* Our Lord had for a long time foreseen the time of His passion. He had, on numerous occasions, predicted it. Yet when it now came clearly into view its terrors exceeded the anticipations of the human Jesus and terrified Him!"[2]

3. In addition to "sorrowful," Matthew also describes Jesus' condition as "very heavy" (26:37). "Again," writes Mitchell, "the word is extremely potent! Some scholars are of the opinion that this emotional shock must have affected His actual physical appearance . . . . Evidently it was at this time that the awareness of Calvary and all it involved came in upon the human Jesus with a traumatic, terrifying jolt which left Him extremely disturbed. The words *sore amazed* and *very heavy* combine to depict a serious emotional state."[3]

4. According to Luke, something actually forced Jesus

onward to prayer; this is indicated by the strong phrase "was withdrawn" (22:41). "Some experts feel it was the very force of His emotions that drove Him. After being withdrawn a short distance Jesus 'fell on his face' (Matt. 26:39). Mark uses a verb tense that indicates repeated or continuous action (see Mark 14:35). Christ was in such emotional anguish that He repeatedly threw Himself to the ground! To say the least the language indicates a desperate struggle.'"[4]

5. Jesus' praying in the garden increased in intensity. When Jesus returned to praying after awakening his sleeping disciples, he was in a state of agony (Luke 22:44). According to Mitchell, this word occurs only here in the New Testament. "The root idea is taken from the struggle and pain of an athletic contest. The full expression, 'being in an agony' (Luke 22:44), conveys the idea of growing intensity. Christ had progressed in struggle from the first prayer into an even more intensive combat.'"[5]

As if the struggle of an athletic contest is not enough to describe what Jesus was going through, Luke says " . . . his sweat was as . . . great drops of blood falling down to the ground" (22:44). A medical doctor says the phenomenon of bloody sweat is well-documented. Under great emotional stress, tiny capillaries in the sweat glands can break, mixing blood and sweat. This process alone is enough to produce weakness and possible shock.

It's hard enough to find words to depict adequately the emotional agony of Jesus. Yet in this intense emotional state, Jesus prayed. "Deep emotions not only prompted prayer, but earnest prayer, for Luke adds that Jesus prayed 'more earnestly.' Heightened emotional distress produced heightened prayer effort! Jesus literally prayed hardest when it was hardest to pray!'"[6]

6. The Gospels depict Jesus' position in prayer differently. Luke describes Jesus as simply kneeling in prayer.

Matthew describes him as prostrate upon the ground, and Mark says Jesus repeatedly fell to the ground. Mitchell says if we combine all three of these, Jesus may have first fallen to his knees then, as the agony grew, literally prostrated himself.

In the height of the prayer struggle, He was in such torment of soul that He was literally writhing in anguish upon the ground. In all probability neither the kneeling nor the prostration were the normal positions Christ assumed while praying. Their very mention and emphasis in this account argues that such behavior appeared unusual to the disciples. They probably had never seen Him conduct Himself in such fashion before. Actually the account indicates that the emotional agony of soul caused Christ to end up prostrate upon the ground . . . He did not assume the kneeling or prostrate positions in order to pray (or even in order to pray more effectively), but rather our Lord, oblivious to His physical position in the intensity of His prayer battle, ended up prostrate upon the ground![7]

Beyond question, Mitchell gives us a graphic portrayal of the struggle Jesus was having. Jesus was approaching the limit of his endurance. That's hard for us to believe. And it's hard to accept this kind of action from the Jesus we know and love and trust. Because it is hard to believe, we look for explanations. How do we explain Jesus' intense, emotional behavior in the garden of Gethsemane?

One explanation of Jesus' emotion is that temptation was at its strongest. Jesus was again facing a way to avoid death. He had been tempted time and again to set up a kingdom that did not involve the cross. His ministry began with that temptation (Mark 1:12-13). What happened in the garden was a renewal of the temptation in the wilderness. Only now, with the cross so near, Satan was putting his all into the fight.

If we find it hard to believe temptation might have caused Jesus such a fierce struggle, we must remember that Jesus experienced temptation like we never have or will. The fact that Jesus was without sin means he knew depths and tensions and assaults of temptation which we will never know. We fall to temptation long before Satan has put out the whole of his power. Jesus' battle with temptation wasn't easier because he was sinless; it was immeasurably harder. In Gethsemane, Jesus struggled with temptation at its fiercest and still did not collapse.

A second explanation, although not a widely accepted one, is the fear of pain. A lot of us don't want to think that the pain and suffering Jesus had to face had anything to do with his prayer for escape in the garden. He was human, we reason, but not that human.

As difficult as it may be for us to accept this explanation, it does contain some truth which we need to consider. It's one thing to talk about dying, to know it is coming; it is another thing to face the actual moment.

Perhaps Jesus had been so concerned with carrying out his mission and training his followers that he had not come to terms with his own suffering and death. Jesus had to cross the brook of Cedron (John 18:1) on his way to the garden. Perhaps there he was starkly reminded of his coming death by the color of the water. It was red from the blood of the lambs slain upon the altar for the Passover. The number of lambs slain was great, probably over two hundred thousand. From the altar where the lambs were slain a channel ran down to the brook Cedron. Through that channel the blood of the Passover lambs drained away. Possibly, as Jesus crossed the brook, the reality of his own blood being shed and the pain that would go with it came in on him in full force. Jesus was a sensitive person who possessed a sense of wonder about this earthly life. His prayer in the garden might have had something to do with a desire to live.

A third explanation for the emotion displayed by Jesus in the garden of Gethsemane might be identification with sin. Johnnie Godwin says, "The persistent prayer of Jesus was for God to remove the need for him to bear the sin of the world in undeserved death. His life was untainted by the sin that separated mankind from God. Jesus looked into the hour and the cup, and he saw the horror of sin that he was to bear."[8] The awful weight of that sin was what was crushing him and causing him such agony.

Temptation at its strongest, fear of pain, weight of sin—here are three possible explanations of the emotional struggle Jesus experienced. Which one is the real explanation? We will probably never know, but we do know the emotion was real.

But how can such emotion come from a person who prayed with such confidence just a short time earlier? Can the two prayers—one of startling confidence and the other of writhing emotion—come from the same person?

The confidence and the emotion were both real—both a part of the same Jesus. Having belief, trust, and confidence in God doesn't take away the emotional involvement that goes along with doing God's will.

When my husband was fired from a job, he gave a confident, I'm-in-control picture to our sons. He came home from work, had a nice meal with the family, and played softball with the boys. As Bob was putting the boys to bed he broke the news to them. I happened to overhear him. "Boys," Bob said, "sometimes your whole world falls in unexpectedly, and it is completely out of our hands to handle it. Daddy lost his job today, but we are going to trust Jesus to see us through and help us find another job." Then he prayed with the boys, as he did each night, and they soon fell asleep, sure that all was well in their world.

I was never prouder of Bob than at that moment. Yet, as I stood listening to him, I knew that in a few minutes I would see another side of Bob. The emotion—the hurt, the shock, the anxiety—would have to be dealt with. There was no sleep for us that night.

Bob was not pretending with the boys. He did trust God, but he also had a lot of emotions that had to be dealt with. Hope and confusion were both there, like the father who brought his demoniac child to be healed. In his tears, he said, "Lord, I believe; help thou mine unbelief" (Mark 9:24). Contradictory emotions can exist side by side.

In his prayer of intercession for his followers, Jesus gave them confidence and hope for the future. He provided them with a cushion of comfort for the bewildering days ahead. When he had completed his task, he went to the garden to deal with his emotions.

The Gospel writer John was there for both occasions. Yet when he looked back to those events, he chose to record the prayer of confidence. The emotion John saw in the garden took nothing away from the prayer of confidence, and neither should it for us.

Knowing that both trust and emotion existed in the life of Jesus should help us. His example helps us know that it is all right to reveal our true emotions in prayer. The writer of Hebrews said that Jesus, in the days of his flesh, offered up his prayers with strong crying and tears (5:7). Jesus, who knew the Father intimately, offered his prayers in this manner. Therefore, we should be honest in our prayers, letting our emotions be what they are.

Karen Burton Mains says she has learned that God is never offended by honest emotions. "How many times he refused to respond to my prayer requests, often for weeks or months. Then when I finally spilled forth my anguished frustrations, suddenly the heavens opened and he overwhelmed me with his love."[9] She says God was doing this to teach her the importance of truth. When she became honest with God, expressing her anger and frustration, then he came in and performed a work of grace.

The honest emotion we express in prayer is to be the emotion of struggle and not the emotion of a spoiled child demanding his way. Emotional prayers are sometimes only the passionate cries of selfish hearts—hearts determined to get what they want. That's not the kind of emotional praying which is appropriate. The struggle which comes when we try to come to grips with the unchangeable certainties in our lives is appropriate. Jesus knew God's will when he prayed this prayer. He was not struggling to discover God's will but to accept it.

The cross for Jesus was both voluntary and essential. In the sense that it was voluntary, escape lay open to him. He need never have come to Jerusalem. He could have compromised with the orthodox Jewish leaders. Regiments of angels were his for his defense if he had wished it so (Matt. 26:51-54).

But, in another sense, escape was not possible for him, not if he wanted to be the obedient Son. The cross was essential to the plan, purpose, and design of God whom Jesus wanted to please. As he came to grips with the necessity of what was before him, he did not *demand* a way out. He *asked* for an escape, but his asking was tempered with "nevertheless not as I will, but as thou *wilt*" (Matt. 26:39).

Within this tension of having to but yet not having to, Jesus asked for an escape. We can too when those unchangeable certainties become more than we can bear. We need to pray and pray, releasing the emotion within us until God's peace replaces it. Then we will be able to carry on. In this way, we have prayers that are both answered sooner and sometimes later. We may not get the answers we want, but God does answer us by giving us the strength to do all along what we knew he wanted.

Jesus did not get the escape he asked for, but he accepted something else in victorious submission. While all of our prayer requests may not be granted in the way we want, they are heard and answered. We may pray for relief from a burden and find instead quiet strength to carry that very burden.

Jesus was given the necessary strength. For him, the emotional battle was won in the garden. Jesus went forth in confidence for all that was to follow. Everything about him and what he did indicated he was in control. The emotional state of Jesus when he entered the garden that night and when he left in chains to later be tried and crucified were entirely different. "Throughout the entire course of the arrest and trial, Jesus was the picture of a man on top of the situation. He displayed tranquility in the midst of turbulence. Something obviously happened in the garden that radically changed the emotional condition of Jesus. *Through prayer* an emotionally disturbed Christ left the garden with quiet confidence to accomplish the Father's will."[9]

This kind of confidence can be ours too. We can pray for an escape when we pray honestly, as Jesus did.

Notes

1. Curtis C. Mitchell, *Praying Jesus' Way* (Old Tappan, New Jersey: Fleming H. Revell, 1977), p. 59.

2. Ibid.

3. Ibid., pp. 59-60.

4. Ibid., p. 61.

5. Ibid., pp. 62-63.

6. Ibid., p. 63.

7. Ibid., p. 65.

8. Johnnie Godwin, *Layman's Bible Book Commentary,* Vol. 16 (Nashville, Tennessee: Broadman Press, 1979), p. 116.

9. Karen Burton Mains, *Karen! Karen!* (Wheaton, Illinois: Tyndale House Publishers, Inc., 1979), p. 54.

10. Curtis C. Mitchell, p. 64.

13 The Ultimate in Forgiving Prayer

After the prayer in the garden of Gethsemane, Jesus was betrayed by Judas, deserted by his friends, and tried before the Jewish Sanhedrin. They turned him over to the Roman governor Pontius Pilate. While being tried by the governor, he was stripped of his clothes, made to wear a crown of thorns, and tormented by Pilate's soldiers. After being rejected by the crowd in favor of the criminal Barabbas, Jesus was nailed to a cross, hoisted up between two thieves. He was left to die a slow and painful death. How did Jesus respond to this humiliating treatment? He responded with a prayer. "Father, forgive them; for they know not what they do" (Luke 23:34).

Surely, such a noble prayer said under such abject circumstances will have much meaning for us, I thought as I began my research. I anxiously read what others had to say about this prayer. To my surprise, instead of finding profound comments about the prayer's spiritual meaning, I found questions. Was this prayer included in the original text of the New Testament? Who was Jesus praying for when he prayed this prayer? And, did God answer this prayer?

To be sure, the oldest and best manuscripts of the New Testament do not include this prayer. It must have been added to the original text. As such, some scholars do not regard this as Jesus' prayer.

Some say Jesus was praying for those who had contributed to his suffering. That would include Peter and the other disciples who fled that night; Pilate; Herod; perhaps Caiaphas, the high priest; and Judas. Others say his prayer was for the Jews who preferred Barabbas over him. Another view says his prayer was asking forgiveness for all people.

If the answer to the second question is forgiveness for everyone, the third question arises. Did God answer his prayer? All men are not forgiven; many die unsaved.

With questions like these being asked about this prayer, it's hard to discern the spiritual truth in it. That's too bad because this prayer has been called the ultimate in forgiving prayer.

A word related to forgiveness is *magnanimity*. It means more that just forgiveness. It means generous in forgiving; the generous part could refer either to the times of forgiving or the amount of injuries that must be forgiven. A magnanimous person is generous in overlooking injury or insult; he is free from petty resentfulness or vindictiveness. Magnanimity suggests greatness of mind or soul, especially as shown in generously overlooking injuries.

The crucifixion was the greatest crime in human history. Whenever the early New Testament preachers spoke of it, a kind of shocked horror was in their voices. The Roman governor himself was well aware that the curcifixion was rank injustice. Jesus did not respond to this injustice with vindictiveness; instead he responded with a prayer asking forgiveness for those who wronged him.

While this prayer may be the ultimate act of forgiveness, Jesus life and teachings show us that magnanimity was a part of his life. He gently treated the adulteress who was about to be stoned (John 8:1-11). In his Sermon on the Mount, he said, "Whosoever shall smite thee on thy right cheek, turn to him the other also," (Matt. 5:39),

"Love your enemies . . . and pray for them which despitefully use you" (Matt. 5:44), and "Judge not, that ye be not judged" (Matt. 7:1). When teaching his followers about prayer, Jesus said, "For if you forgive men their trespasses, your heavenly Father will also forgive you: But if you forgive not men their trespasses, neither will your Father forgive your trespasses" (Matt. 6:14-15). Such words were not hollow advice; Jesus' life and death superbly demonstrated his teachings. Whether the words "Father, forgive them" were actually uttered from the cross, the prayer is in line with the mind of Christ.

Jesus' act of dying was a prayer that was asking forgiveness for every person. Jesus died so everyone could know God's forgiveness. In that sense, his prayer—whether act or words—was and is answered. Forgiveness was provided by Jesus' death on the cross. This does not mean that the forgiven automatically enter into a right relationship with God, but it does mean forgiveness was made possible. Each individual must decide whether he will receive it. Jesus' first prayer from the cross reveals the deepest will and purpose of God; therefore, we can be certain the prayer was heard and answered. Forgiveness is available for all.

For most of us, however, our problem will not be in determining whether the words were actually said from the cross or whether the prayer was really answered. Our difficulty will be in trying to be like Jesus. The Gospels make it plain that Jesus intended for those who follow him to be magnanimous.

The magnanimous response is not easy. When we feel sorely wronged, our first impulse is to strike back. Jesus' prayer, however, gives us a clue to help us. The clue is in the words, "for they know not what they do." Understanding those words gives us insight on how we can be magnanimous.

For those of us who love Jesus, we can't help but ask, How did those who crucified him not know what they were doing? As we read and study the Gospels, Jesus' crucifixion seems like a deliberate, well-planned execution. If anything, it looks like they knew exactly what they were doing. There were, of course, those at the foot of the cross who were totally ignorant of what was going on. It was simply their job to be there.

But Jesus looked upon others at the foot of the cross, those who willfully put him to death, and saw them as victims of a system. They were blinded by the ceremonial restrictions of the law. They were blinded by years of tradition of what they perceived God to be like. Jesus saw them responding to the forces around them. They were unaware of the dreadful consequences of their act. They did not know that they were bringing suffering and death to the One who was "the image of the invisible God" (Col. 1:15).

The lesson is clear. If we wish to be magnanimous, we must look with understanding eyes at the persons who hurt us. What forces shaped their lives? What drove them to do what they did? If we could know all that is in cruel people's hearts, we might be more tender in our judgments. Here are some examples of some people who were able to see beyond their own hurt.

(1) Carol's friends say she is a saint in comparison to her husband. Through the years, they've watched her care for him, keep his home for him, and be a devoted wife and companion. Tom seems totally oblivious to all of her virtues, often making her the butt of his public jokes. He seldom shows her any kindness or gentleness.

How does Carol go on caring for him without ever receiving any kindness in return? Her continual prayer is, "God, forgive him, for he knows not what he does." Carol knows her husband well. She is aware of his poor upbringing. She is aware that he was never taught how to show appreciation or how to lovingly treat a wife. She's also sensitive to his fierce pride that will not allow him to admit his insensitivity or admit his need for counseling. She loves him and accepts him because she knows from whence he came and knows what is inside him keeps him from changing.

(2) Ted and Shirley were in their early fifties when they realized how much their church needed someone to work with the youth of their church on a volunteer basis. They volunteered. They had the youth in their home for planning sessions, gave them lots of leeway in planning with just the right amount of firm guidance, and even made trips out of town to purchase needed supplies. Things were going well until a much younger couple joined the church. This couple was very attractive, dressed much like the youth, and talked a lot. Their youthful appearance and talkativeness held a natural charisma for the youth. The new members soon let the youth know what they would do if they were the Youth directors. The kids listened and soon became discontented with Ted's and Shirley's leadership. Eventually, Ted and Shirley were forced to resign, and the young couple became the new Youth directors.

How did Ted and Shirley cope with their hurt of being tossed aside after so much work on their part? They prayed, "God, forgive them for they know not what they do. We understand how easily persuaded youth can be. We understand they are not able to discern what kind of leaders they really need."

(3) In the summer of 1964, when outbreaks of fighting were increasing in the Congo (now Zaire), missionary Joe Tucker and his family returned to the Congo. They had been on furlough in the United States. They returned to their place of service against the counsel of their friends. Tucker had served twenty-five years in the Congo and was

very proficient in the native languages and translated many books into Swahili. Through his help, twenty schools, one a college, had been started.

Within a few weeks of their return their village was captured by the rebels and they were seized along with other missionaries. On the day before Thanksgiving, as rescue forces neared their village, Mr. Tucker was dragged from his place of confinement and beaten to death. According to witnesses to his execution, it was not a quick and merciful death. The beating took forty-five minutes, one blow at a time, with each new blow only falling after his groaning from the previous blow had ceased.

When reporters spoke to Mrs. Tucker after the rescue of her and her children, the only comment she had was, "I understand why these things happen."

Louis Cassels, the UPI writer who reported this story, commented, "In that simple, compassionate sentence you can hear quite clearly the echo of another voice speaking from the cross: 'Father, forgive them; for they know not what they do.' "[1]

The magnanimous response to people who hurt us does not condone wrongdoing. It was not right for Joe Tucker to be murdered, for the youth to turn against Shirley and Ted when a younger couple came along, or for Tom to treat Shirley the way he does. The early New Testament preachers tried to impress upon people the sheer crime of the cross. Magnanimity does not suggest that wrongdoers go scot-free, but it does call for understanding the pressures that lead to the wrongdoing. When we do, we'll be on our way to forgiving, and we'll be able to pray as Jesus did: "Father, forgive them; for they know not what they do."

Notes

1. James M. Lapp, "The Word of Forgiveness," *The Way of the Cross and Resurrection*, John M. Drescher, ed. (Scottdale, Pennsylvania: Herald Press, 1978), pp. 121-122.

14 The Mysterious Prayer

We have seen Jesus writhing with intense emotion over God's will, and we have seen him dealing with his persecutors and tormentors with a prayer of forgiveness. Surely, we think, in these two experiences, he penetrated the depths of emotions. But not so. From the cross rang a cry of such utter abandonment that we are tempted to turn away and to cover our ears to keep from hearing what he said.

For almost six hours, Jesus hung on the cross. The last half of those hours were spent in darkness. During those three hours of darkness, Jesus was silent. Doubtless, he suffered extreme anguish of spirit, as well as physical pain. The agonies of the crucifixion were deepening more and more as death neared. Forsaken by men, he felt isolated and alone.

Near the end of the three hours of darkness, feeling forsaken by God, Jesus cried out in the awful stillness of the darkness. *"Eloi, Eloi, lama sabachthani?* (Mark 15:34). This Aramaic cry is translated "My God, my God, why hast thou forsaken me?" Without a doubt, this statement has to be one of the most staggering in the Gospel record. The cry reveals suffering far greater than just the physical pain of the crucifixion. A crushing grief, even greater than that experienced in Gethsemane, was expressed in this cry.

We cannot fathom such a cry coming from the lips of Jesus after seeing the perfect communion he had with the Father. And, too, the prayer scares us because God is our one reliance. He is the One on whom we depend to always be with us (Deut. 31:6; Josh. 1:5; and Heb. 13:5). We wonder, if Jesus could be forsaken, does that mean we, too, could be forsaken?

The prayer is a mystery because of the break we see in the closeness of the Father and the Son, and the implications it has for us. Many attempts have been made to penetrate behind the mystery of this prayer. Here are three of the more common ones.

1. *Jesus was repeating Scripture.* The words of this prayer are taken directly from Psalm 22. This Psalm runs through the whole crucifixion narrative, and Jesus' prayer is actually the first verse of that Psalm.

There was good reason for Jesus to be reminded of Psalm 22. As the executioners claimed his clothing as their right, he recalled, "They part my garments among them, and cast lots upon my vesture" (Ps. 22:18). Also, the scoffing and mocking of the chief priests, scribes, and elders brought to mind another passage of Psalm 22: "All they that see me laugh me to scorn: they shoot out the lip, they shake the head, *saying,* He trusted on the Lord *that* he would deliver him; let him deliver him, seeing he delighted in him" (v. 7-8).

As these events happened around Jesus, Psalm 22 came to his mind, and some of it was expressed in his prayer. The Psalm is a picture of a forsaken and besieged person; he has unshaken confidence in God's goodness and in his final dominion over all nations. Because the Psalm is a song of trust and confidence which begins in complete despair and ends in soaring triumph, some insist Jesus' prayer was not an expression of doubt. Rather, they look at the prayer as evidence that Jesus died as he lived, with God's

Word on his lips and with unshaken trust in him who alone and always is our true help.

"That is an attractive suggestion," says William Barclay, "but on a cross a man does not repeat poetry to himself, even the poetry of a psalm."[1] More than likely, Jesus felt that God had abandoned him to his tragic cup of destiny; and he remembered the cry of the psalmist. In that tortured moment, the cry became his own.

2. *Jesus was made sin.* Henry Burto of *The Expositor's Bible* says we can interpret the mysterious prayer of Jesus in but one way. The Lamb of God was bearing the sin of the world. He was taking for men the bitter pains of the second death, and as he drank the cup of the wrath of God against sin he felt passing over him the awful loneliness of a soul bereft of God. He felt the chill of the "outer darkness" itself.

Up to this moment Jesus had gone through every experience of life except one: separation from God because of sin. Jesus had taken this life of ours upon himself. He had done our work and faced our temptations and borne our trials. He had suffered all that life could bring to him. He had known the failure of friends, the hatred of foes, the malice of enemies. He had known the most searing pain that life can offer, but he had never known the consequence of sin.

Sin separates us from God. It puts up between us and God a barrier that is like an unscalable wall. Jesus had never experienced that because he was without sin. Perhaps that experience came upon him as the weight of the world's sin fell upon his heart and being. It was in that moment when he who knew no sin was made sin for us (2 Cor. 5:21).

This separation from God did not come because Jesus had sinned. It came because Jesus really and truly identified himself with the sin of humanity. He felt acutely the weight of the burden which was his as he took on the sins of the whole world. In that moment, he knew what it meant to be a sinner. This experience must have been doubly agonizing for him because he had never known what it was to be separated from God by sin. His fellowship with God, which had always sustained him, was briefly clouded; and his prayer reveals just how awful that was for him.

3. *Jesus was plumbing the depths of human experience.* The word *forsaken* gives the impression that Jesus felt the Father was not present in the sense in which he had always been. Jesus' prayer expressed the wretched feeling of temporarily broken fellowship. This was his only taste of broken communion.

This explanation is like to the previous one. They both stress broken fellowship. The two views differ as to the cause for the broken communion. One says sin is the explanation; the other one says loneliness. If we think about it, the loneliness must have been painful.

The crowd, instead of being moved to compassion by His suffering, were either idly curious or openly glad that He was in torment. Instead of compassion which He needed at this point, He received ridicule. Many apparently thought that His claims had been too great, and now they were glad to see Him brought low.[2]

The cowardly actions of his followers accentuated his loneliness. "Where were the Twelve to whom He had given His closest attention? Where were the members of the innermost circle, once gathered for prayer on the Mountain of Transfiguration?"[3]

Jesus had known sorrow and tears. Our study of his prayer life has revealed that Jesus expressed many emotions. We have seen him disappointed, frustrated, weary, bereaved, rejected, and suffering. Millard Osborne, says the loneliness on the cross was more painful than anything else that had happened in Jesus' earthly life.

The most acute kind of loneliness is not caused by the absence of other persons. It is the aloneness that engulfs us when we are unable to sense that others are sharing, caring, supporting, or identifying with us in a time of great need. To be in the midst of people and not be able to sense that others know, or care to know, what is happening inside you—that is a loneliness which separates and isolates.[4]

This kind of loneliness coupled with feeling forsaken by God, can send one plummeting to the depths of human experience. Fortunately this kind of experience is not the norm of life. But bitter tragedy does enter our lives. Those are times when we feel God and everyone else have forsaken us. That is what happened to Jesus. In the garden of Gethsemane, Jesus knew he had to go on because that was God's will, and he struggled to accept it. Here we see Jesus plumbing the uttermost depths of life so that we would not have to go where he has not been before us.

Which of these three explanations is the real one for the mysterious prayer? Quoting Scripture? Bearing the sin of the world? Plumbing the depths of human experience? We don't know; we can only surmise, considering them all as possibilities. If one is true or if all three are true, they offer some very real help for us.

If the explanation that Jesus was repeating Scripture, we have an example of what to do in difficult moments. Jesus' life was rooted in and nourished by the rich, fertile soil of the Old Testament. From his childhood, Jesus studied the Old Testament, and its words worked their way into his personality.

The Old Testament was indispensable to Jesus' life of devotion and communion with the Father. The Bible is indispensable to us if we want to develop and nourish our devotional lives. That is why sayings from the Old Testament later leapt spontaneously to his mind and become an integral part of the triumphs he won. The critical moments of his earthly ministry—reflect the attitude and poise of spirit of one whose mind was steeped in the Old Testament.

Some parts of the Old Testament were favored by Jesus. These he used in the critical moments of his life. He often quoted from Isaiah and the Psalms, as we have seen in his prayer of abandonment. In the wilderness temptations (Matt. 4:1-11; Mark 1:12-13; and Luke 4:1-13), Jesus used the words of Deuteronomy to answer each temptation. He quoted Deuteronomy 8:3 when tempted to make bread. Deuteronomy 6:13 answered the temptation to power, and the temptation to engage in spectacular acts was answered by Deuteronomy 6:16.

If the correct explanation is that Jesus were made sin, if he did suffer that awful desolation of being separated from God, we need never fear going to him when sin cuts us off from God. Sin is like an unscalable wall separating us from the presence of God. It so separates us that we begin to think God doesn't care, that he wouldn't answer even if we were to pray. But Jesus understands. He knows how we feel. He felt the way sinners feel; therefore, we need never fear going to him and asking him to plead our case with the Father when sin cuts us off from God.

If Jesus were plumbing the depths, we can have great comfort when we feel abandoned. The difference between this explanation and the second one is that one is caused by us and the other isn't. We can let sin build up in our lives until we are separated from God and feel abandoned. That kind of abandonment is the result of our doing.

But we are not directly responsible for the abandonment in this third explanation. The death of someone near to us or an accident that brings an abrupt change to our life can bring feelings of abandonment. It may not be an experience all Christians share. Some do experience it, however.

C. S. Lewis experienced it after the death of his wife. He described his feelings of abandonment by God as "a door slammed in your face, and a sound of bolting and double bolting on the inside."[5]

One Christian, trying to recover from an injustice done to her, could seem to get no guidance whatsoever from God. She said,

I feel like Becky Thatcher and Tom Sawyer when they were lost in the cave along the Mississippi river. Their candles had burned out, and they needed to find their way out. With nothing but darkness and caverns all around them, Tom was afraid to venture too far from Becky for fear of where he would step. He tied a string about himself and tied it near her and ventured out, feeling his way in the darkness. He would wave his arms out in front of him to see if there was anything in front of him. He would reach his hand around a wall to see what was around the corner. He would stick a foot out into space to see if there was anything solid to stand on. He would drop a rock and listen for it to hit bottom to see how deep the crevice in front of him was. All the time it would have been so much easier if he had had a candle to see by.

I feel that way. No matter which way I step, I'm afraid I'm going to fall. In the darkness, I'm trying to find a sure place to stand. If God would just give me some guidance . . . a candle to light my way, how much easier it would be.

What do these experiences mean? If some Christians feel abandonment, if Jesus experienced it, does that mean we are abandoned by God? No, the feeling and the fact may not be the same thing. While we may never understand the why behind this mysterious prayer of Jesus', we do know that God did not abandon him during this time. God's purpose was still in operation. *The Broadman Bible Commentary* says, "God did not turn his back on Jesus, as some theology has it. God was never nearer than at Golgotha, as Jesus gave himself in full obedience to the Father's will."[6]

Events around the cross convince us that God did not abandon Jesus. What nature did at this time shows us God's heart. Jesus' death was so terrible that the sky was unnaturally darkened, as if nature could not bear to look. Death came in a short time. This was a surprise to all; death on the cross was death by slow exhaustion and could take days. After Jesus' cry of abandonment, death came. It was as if God were saying, "The cross may be necessary, but I'll not have you suffer any longer than is necessary."

Jesus died with a shout of triumph on his lips. He gave a victorious shout (Matt. 27:50; Mark 15:37; Luke 23:46), and the shout was, "It is finished" (John 19:30). In the Greek, that would have been one word: "Finished!" It was the shout of a man who had completed the task, a man who had won through the struggle, a man who had come out of darkness into light. Jesus died with the cry of triumph on his lips, his task accomplished, his work completed, his victory won. After the terrible dark of abandonment, there came the light again, and Jesus died a victor.

Jesus had passed through the uttermost abyss, whether that was separation from God by the weight of sin or by the depths of loneliness. He was the victor. He cried out his desperation to God, and God came to him on the cross and ended Jesus' ordeal with victory. If there could be a more reassuring conclusion, what would it be?

Notes

1. William Barclay, *The Gospel of Matthew*, Vol. 2, Revised (Edinburgh, Scotland: The Saint Andrew Press, 1975), pp. 406-407.

2. Elton Trueblood, The Lord's Prayer, pp. 121-122.

3. Ibid., p. 122.

4. Millard Osborne, "The Word of Loneliness," *The Way of the Cross and Resurrection* edited by John M. Drescher (Scottdale, Pennsylvania: Herald Press, 1978), p. 157.

5. C. S. Lewis, *A Grief Observed* (New York, New York: The Seabury Press, 1961), p. 9.

6. *The Broadman Bible Commentary*, Vol. 8 (Nashville, Tennessee: Broadman Press, 1970), p. 246.

15 A Prayer of Commitment

After his prayer of abandonment, fellowship was restored between Jesus and the Father. Jesus finished the work God had given him. He bowed his head and willed to give up his spirit, sending it back to the Father. "And Jesus, crying out with a loud voice, said, 'Father, into Thy hands I commit My spirit.' And having said this, He breathed His last" (Luke 23:46, NASB).

This prayer, like the last one, is a quotation from the Psalms. "Into thine hand I commit my spirit" from Psalm 31:5 was often used by Jews as a prayer of commitment. To these words, Jesus added one word, "Father."

This prayer of commitment was the first prayer every Jewish mother taught her child to say when he lay down to sleep at night. Mary had probably taught the prayer to Jesus. When he was dying, Jesus prayed the prayer he had prayed many times as a little boy.

Following the prayer on the cross, Jesus bowed his head and died. The word which John used to say that Jesus bowed his head is the word for a man peacefully letting his head sink back upon his pillow to go to sleep (John 19:30). So peace came to Jesus after his long battle, rest after his earnest work, and contentment knowing he had completed his task. With the sure and restful sigh of a tired child, Jesus died. He died confident of his Father's care.

Jesus' last prayer is a beautiful and helpful one. It

shows us how to live and how to die. Some have faced death screaming and cursing. Some have faced it with grim resignation, but Jesus showed us how to face it appropriately—with a sense of completion and peace.

On the cross, during the silent intervals, Jesus must have reflected on his life. Flashes of his boyhood and the sense of mission which always lay upon him must have come to his mind. He remembered his years of teaching, serving, and spiritual travail. He remembered those times on the mountain slopes, times of communion and refreshment with the Father. Now all he had done, had sought, hoped for, and dreamed about was finished. He had accomplished what the Father had called him to do. What Jesus had been, done, and sought had brought him to the cross, and he had endured. His work was finished. All that he could do had been done; all that he could give had been given.

There are not too many things we do in this life about which we can truthfully say, It is finished. We do not have enough time to do everything that must be done. Or, we are not conscientious enough. Or, we have so many tasks that none are done well. Seldom do we experience moments in which we can lay down our tools, wipe our hands, and say, "I have done this job with all the power and ability I have. I have not consciously left any part of it undone. It is finished."

If it is hard to experience a sense of completeness in this life, it would be harder at death unless we knew what we wanted to accomplish. What is my purpose here on earth? What kind of life do I want to live so that when death is near, I can look back and know I gave everything I had to give? Jesus knew where he was going. From his first prayer, he knew his mission and his destiny; he could die knowing he had achieved what God wanted him to achieve. Perhaps we need to take stock of our living so that we may die appropriately. Contemplative prayer can help us do that. "Father, show your will to me, what you want me to accomplish, so I may die with the sense of completion that Jesus died with."

Along with this sense of completeness for Jesus was also a sense of peace. While a rupture in his relationship with God did occur on the cross, it was restored prior to his dying. He died as a child going to sleep at night, assured of his Father's care.

The word the King James Version of the Bible uses in this prayer for commit is *commend*. This word means to entrust, to deliver with confidence, to give as a deposit for trust or safekeeping. Jesus was obedient all through his life; and now, even though he had experienced the cross and abandonment, he was ready to deposit his life into the hands of God for whatever the future held.

Jesus expressed this confidence with a prayer. Does this surprise us? We have seen him praying in all the significant moments in his life. We should not be surprised that he met death in the same way he met life. His prayer life has shown us his dependence upon God and how much prayer meant to him. It is wonderfully appropriate that his last utterance was one of commitment and that it was in the form of prayer.

Jesus' final prayer not only shows us how to die but it also shows us how to live. The key word is *commit*. Jesus' greatest call was a call to commitment when he said, "Come unto me . . . Take my yoke upon you" (Matt. 11:28-29).

Commitment is more than mere belief. It is more than acknowledging the existence of God. It includes involvement, risk, and courage. It means the determination to live and act in light of what we know to be true. To have that kind of determination calls for depositing our wills and our spirits in God's hands.

Jesus was committed to the Father's will. Throughout Jesus' life, he was the obedient Son. Nevertheless, his prayer life has shown us that he struggled with God's will. Praying helped him with the struggle, but prayer never took away the struggle once and for all. From the very first prayer, Jesus knew he was on his way to the cross. His concept of what all that meant increased throughout his ministry, but his destiny never changed. Jesus' dying on the cross was a voluntary act but in another sense, it wasn't. If he wanted to be the obedient Son, there was only one way before him.

We, too, struggle with God's will. The struggle may come in response to God's call to a particular task or vocation, or the struggle may come in having to face a certainty in life that cannot be changed. Here is how Jesus' example in prayer can help us with our struggles.

1. Jesus used prayer to align his will with the Father's. Jesus knew God's will, and he prayed to accept it. For some of us, praying may be a matter of finding out what God's will is for us. Others of us may know what it is and not want to do it. Prayer will enable us to align our wills with God's. "Father, into thy hands, I commit my will."

2. Jesus was honest in expressing his struggle, and he taught his followers to pray honestly and naturally. He made no pretense, no cover-up. He did not repress his feelings. "Father, now is my soul troubled."

3. Jesus prayed for direction in doing God's will. Knowing God's will and doing it are two different things. Choices have to be made. Relationships have to be considered. Doing God's will, once we know it, is never a simple thing. More choices will be called for, and other people will be affected. "Father, into thy hands, I commit my choices and my relationships."

4. Jesus prayed for escape. It is not wrong to pray for an escape when we really pray to God. Some of our prayers

are merely our own insistence on what we think has to be. By praying for escape, with our hearts open to God, we can free ourselves of the negative emotion of the situation and let God's peace fill us. "Nevertheless, not my will, but thine be done."

5. Jesus prayed for strength. Jesus withdrew for time alone with the Father in order to refresh his Spirit. This enabled him to carry on. God doesn't expect us to do his will without help. He wants to help and will when we open our spirits to him through prayer for refreshment. "Father, into thy hands, I commit my spirit."

6. Jesus prayed to give thanks. Jesus' prayers must always be interpreted in light of the cross, that unchangeable certainty in his life. But the cross must always be interpreted in light of the resurrection. Jesus did not stay on the cross. Release from his long struggle came in the form of the resurrection, giving purpose and meaning to all he had been through. Jesus' resurrection appearance to the disciples opened their minds to understand the Scriptures (Luke 24:45). Understanding of our unchangeable certainties will eventually come. (Luke 24:50-53). We'll see what we've been through as blessed and see how God was in it all. "Thank you, Father, for so it seemed good in thy sight."

Jesus' final prayer helps us know how to die and how to live. In both cases, it is a matter of commitment—trusting our lives, our wills, and our spirits to his care. Commitment is never easy, but it can be done when we learn to pray as Jesus prayed.